Advance Praise for

Global Profit *AND* Global Justice

Deb Abbey has done it again! This informative and
comprehensive introduction to investing for positive
social change is a marvelous resource for all, whether a new
investor or a seasoned one. Weaving together specific
examples and how-to advice, Ms. Abbey builds a case for hope.
Consumers, investors, activists and — yes — even caring
business leaders are emerging to join together in
building a better tomorrow for all.

— AMY DOMINI, Founder, CEO & President,
Domini Social Investments

Global Profit and Global Justice was a delightful read and
very much like going through a gift basket of wonderful
foods — juicy, nutritious, energizing and something you
don't want to end. I found it to be a reference, a reminder
and a great resource. I want to have this book near
me when I work on these big daunting issues.
Its reasonable and balanced approach was refreshing
and the information that was contained within the
pages truly rewarding. Thanks for giving me the
opportunity to learn more, understand deeper, and
become more empathetic to the complicated issues.
But thanks very, very much for bringing
the AND into play instead of the OR.

— MARGOT FRANSSEN OC, President, The Body Shop Canada

People feel increasingly helpless in the face of the continuing onslaught of globalization. This important book provides proof and practical examples of how we can change the world through our spending, investments and charitable giving.

— MICHAEL JANTZI, President, Michael Jantzi Research Associates Inc., Canada's leading social research providers.

Global Profit AND Global Justice is about hope and about how you can make a difference. As a consumer, as an investor, as a person, your individual choices matter. When you make informed choices, and align them with those of caring people in your community and around the world, you shift the terms of the global economy.

— JOEL SOLOMON, from the foreword

For Brendon,
Warmest regards.
Deb Abbey

GLOBAL PROFIT *And* GLOBAL JUSTICE

Using Your
Money to
Change the
World

DEB ABBEY

with PERRY ABBEY, TIM DRAIMIN, ADINE MEES AND CORO STRANDBERG

NEW SOCIETY PUBLISHERS

Cataloguing in Publication Data:
A catalog record for this publication is available from the National Library of
Canada.

Cover design by Diane McIntosh. Image: Photodisc RF.

Printed in Canada by Transcontinental.

New Society Publishers acknowledges the support of the Government of
Canada through the Book Publishing Industry Development Program (BPIDP)
for our publishing activities.

Paperback ISBN: 0-86571-502-5

Inquiries regarding requests to reprint all or part of *Global Profit AND Global
Justice* should be addressed to New Society Publishers at the address below.

To order directly from the publishers, please add $4.50 shipping to the price of
the first copy, and $1.00 for each additional copy (plus GST in Canada). Send
check or money order to:

New Society Publishers
P.O. Box 189, Gabriola Island, BC V0R 1X0, Canada
1-800-567-6772

New Society Publishers' mission is to publish books that contribute in fundamental ways to building an ecologically sustainable and just society, and to do
so with the least possible impact on the environment, in a manner that models
this vision. We are committed to doing this not just through education, but
through action. We are acting on our commitment to the world's remaining
ancient forests by phasing out our paper supply from ancient forests worldwide.
This book is one step towards ending global deforestation and climate change.
It is printed on acid-free paper that is **100% old growth forest-free** (100%
post-consumer recycled), processed chlorine free, and printed with vegetable
based, low VOC inks. For further information, or to browse our full list of
books and purchase securely, visit our website at: www.newsociety.com

NEW SOCIETY PUBLISHERS   www.newsociety.com

DEDICATION

To my Dad, Micky, who has encouraged me to take on huge challenges and never to give up on them, to take my vitamins, and to ask my partners for a raise because he's sure they couldn't possibly be paying me enough. I love you, Dad. I'm sorry I didn't make it to medical school.

To my family — my husband Perry, my daughters Brooke and Brenna, and my son-in-law, Joseph. In Brooke's words: we put the *fun* back in dysfunctional.

CONTENTS

ACKNOWLEDGMENTS

Thank you, Renewal Partners, for sharing my dream of leveraging capital for social change. Thank you Carol Newell and Joel Solomon and Martha Burton. And thanks to my good friend and business partner, Deb Elliott.

A very special thanks to Jamie Bonham. Jamie is a brilliant researcher and this book could not have been written without his contributions.

To my team at Real Assets for their support and assistance in getting this book to the publisher. Adam Ho, Sean Kelly, Indi Shoker, and Lynn Shook are the brightest, most talented, and loyal group of people I've ever known.

To my guest authors — Tim Draimin, Adine Mees, Drummond Pike, and Coro Strandberg. They are change agents in this world. To my husband Perry Abbey who contributed two chapters and helped with the book at every stage and to my daughter Brooke Abbey who is a great editor.

To Sonja Reid for top-notch research, Kai Alderson for sifting through stacks of academic studies, and Amy Stein for her valuable contribution to the philanthropy chapter.

To my partners in social change, VanCity and United Capital. In particular I want to thank Bruce Ralston (and the VanCity board of directors), Dave Mowat, David Levi and Brian Worth.

To Chris and Judith Plant and everyone at New Society Publishing for being part of the solution!

To my sister Patty Meeker and my best friend Viki Jackson for their friendship and for reading parts of the manuscript and saying, "Have you thought of writing a mystery instead?" and "It's not really boring at all."

And to the GDs and GTGs. You know who you are and you know what you did!

FOREWORD

BY JOEL SOLOMON

This book is a tonic for that knot of despair in the pit of your stomach. We all feel it, growing tighter every time we confront the harsh realities of poverty, injustice and environmental degradation, the common by-products of our globalized economy.

Global Profit AND Global Justice is about hope and about how you can make a difference. As a consumer, as an investor, as a person, your individual choices matter. When you make informed choices, and align them with those of caring people in your community and around the world, you shift the terms of the global economy.

Each of the contributors to this book has decades of experience on the cutting edge of social change. They are honest about the tough challenges that lie ahead, but face them with a steadfast, constructive optimism. They chronicle many of the victories already achieved through consumer and shareholder campaigns.

My role as a founding partner and CEO of Renewal Partners Company has been devoted to capitalizing and building high social-impact business ventures. My role in the Endswell Foundation and Tides Canada Foundation launches has been about funding and building practical tools for helping people give away money to progressive social change charities. Through this work I've had the privilege to meet and work with some of North America's leading social entrepreneurs.

When we launched our entities, I looked around the city for someone who was familiar with social screening of managed money. The only name I heard everywhere I went was Deb Abbey. Knowing I had to meet this person, I was delighted to find such a committed and determined woman. No one could convince her that aligning money with social impact was anything other than obvious and would soon be the dominant theme in all portfolios. I was drawn to Deb's vision and her ability to make success out of impossible challenges. When she said she wanted to start a new company, focused entirely on social impact investing, tough as that sounded, I could only smile and sign on. When she brought VanCity into the mix, I knew she was on the road to even bigger impact.

As an innovative pioneer in Canada's financial industry, she is one of my favorite thinkers. She's a bold risk-taker on behalf of societal purpose and values, while establishing an enterprise that is changing the way money is managed.

Perry Abbey is a good friend, manages my personal accounts, and leads the way in tailoring to the values of the individual, able to navigate the many different investments out there, with humor and savvy.

The launch of Tides Canada required a perfect executive director. Who could provide a national scope and broad understanding of social and environmental issues? Who had the personality to help bring alive the funding agendas of clients, while fitting all those agendas into a cohesive societal context? Finding Tim Draimin was the key to the formula. He's led Tides Canada far beyond what we originally thought possible.

Drummond Pike is one of my oldest friends and an important mentor. I've been a client and board member of the Tides Foundation for many years. Tides Canada was inspired through my association with Drummond. Renewal Partners has been a founding member of Canadian Business for Social Responsibility. Adine Mees is a long time colleague and collaborator, renowned for her strategic vision and systematic organizational building. Coro Strandberg was one of the first people I met when I moved to Vancouver. Her commitment to the emerging social investment sector in Canada has been unwavering.

In this book, Deb and her guest authors look ahead to show how enlightened investors, through their mutual funds and pension funds, are prompting a new breed of business leaders to embrace the principles of corporate social responsibility. How progressive companies are racing to introduce disruptive technologies that are going to change the direction of history. How a burgeoning community investing movement is addressing the needs of people previously bypassed by the globalized economy.

Money is powerful. We can use our money power. We can direct our dollars where they will work for a just and sustainable economy. As millions of us take responsibility for the impact of who and what our dollars support, we are the seeds of the next great social movement. Together, with committed minds and hearts, we can build the world we want.

GLOBAL PROFIT AND GLOBAL JUSTICE

The world is not dangerous because of those who do harm, but because of those who look at it without doing anything.

— Albert Einstein

WHAT IF YOU WOKE UP one day and the world just wasn't the same?

That day has come and gone. A UN report forecasts that, without intervention, 129 million people in Africa will die of HIV/AIDS by the year 2015 and 480 million by 2050. And two out of every three people on Earth won't have access to clean water by the year 2025, and so on. The world is heading for a future that none of us hoped for — unless we take action now.

It's easy to envision the nightmare scenarios, but it's important not to be consumed by them. This book is about hope. We remain in control of our destiny and we must believe that it's not too late to change course. All we need is for like-minded people to come together for a common cause. The cause is the survival of our planet and all the life it encompasses.

Our crisis is that we've lost faith in our governments to lead, lost faith in our capitalist system to provide for us in a fair and equitable manner, and lost faith in our ability to have any impact at all on the outcome of either. And if government does not lead, then who will? Increasingly, it's corporations that determine policies and practices at home and abroad. Some people think that globalization is evil, but the reality is that it's probably inevitable. Instead of fighting globalization, I propose that we spend our energy creating a vibrant global community with a sustainable environment and justice for all.

I wrote this book because I believe that each of us can make choices in our daily lives that will shape the future of globalization over the next ten, twenty or fifty years. We have options. We have to think big, start small, and act now. Margaret Mead, the world's most famous anthropologist, said, "Never doubt that a small group of thoughtful, committed citizens can change the world. Indeed it's the only thing that ever has." Those words have never been more relevant than they are today. We have to start somewhere.

When I started my career in the investment business ten years ago, it didn't occur to me to pursue anything other than social impact investing. I had always made decisions that were consistent with my personal values — and social impact investing was simply an extension of those values. But over the years I realized that it wasn't only about the values that were important to me. None of us believe in child slavery or sweatshop labor or environmental degradation, and all of us want to live in strong, sustainable communities.

In 2000 I launched Real Assets Investment Management so that I could help individual and institutional investors leverage their capital for social change. Along the way, it became clear that we would need multiple strategies to change the world. This book will introduce you to a number of these approaches, beginning with investigating the role of the individual and expanding out to include ways the individual can act in concert with others to broaden the impact.

My guest authors are just a few of the amazing people that I've had the pleasure of collaborating with over the years. Each of them brings unique experiences in leveraging money for social change.

Perry Abbey, my husband and an investment advisor specializing in social impact investing, has been constructing model portfolios of cutting edge companies for many years. Coro Strandberg is a long-time advocate of building strong sustainable communities through community investing. Adine Mees has been a leading advocate of corporate social responsibility through her work in the corporate and nonprofit sectors. And Tim Draimin and Drummond Pike are continuously breaking new ground in the philanthropic community, helping mission-driven social investors craft donor strategies that promote positive change in the world. We must make a reality of our vision of global profit in the context of global justice. This book is a handbook of strategies for that change.

FROM PRIVATE GREEN TO PUBLIC GOOD

A poll conducted in 1999 by Environics for the Prince of Wales Business Leaders Forum and The Conference Board shows a number of interesting trends in attitudes towards companies. The Millennium Poll interviewed 25,000 citizens in 23 countries on their opinions of corporate social responsibility.

In terms of power and influence, you can forget about the church, forget politics. There is no more powerful institution in society than business .... The business of business should not be about money, it should be about responsibility. It should be about public good, not private greed.
— Anita Roddick, Business as Unusual[1]

- Fifty-six percent of people responded that they formed their opinions of a company based on its social and environmental responsibility, ahead of brand reputation and business fundamentals
- Forty-three percent of Canadians, 39 percent of the British, and 35 percent of Americans feel that the role of large companies in society is to set higher ethical standards and help build a better society.
- In North America and Australia/New Zealand, 51 percent had punished a company in the last year for not being socially responsible.

And a 2003 Environics poll found that 80 percent of Canadian respondents stated they were willing to pay more to buy socially or environmentally responsible products, and 66 percent said they would pay more if the company donates to charity. Among shareholders, 52 percent believe that a company's social and environmental performance is as important as its financial performance, while 88 percent said that companies should pay more attention to ethical factors.

These statistics reveal a profoundly optimistic vision of change. One in which the needs of the markets and of society merge, so that people power can shape economic forces to make the world a better place.

WHAT IS GLOBALIZATION?

The concept of globalization is characterized by a lot of debate and little consensus. In other words, everybody talks about it, but not everyone is talking about the same thing. This is especially true when you try to understand its effects on real people.

The Coffee Question

Let's look at the impact globalization has had on the international coffee market. Like many commodities, coffee used to be traded in a managed market, regulated by the International Coffee Agreement. Governments of producing and consuming nations cooperated to keep the price relatively stable. In the late '80s this system of managed trade broke down. Since then, prices for coffee have been determined on the futures markets in London and New York. As a result, prices have become far more volatile than before and have generally dropped much lower than they were prior to liberalization of the international coffee market.

The problem is oversupply. The volume of coffee produced far exceeds the demand. Supply has been growing at more than two percent while demand has only been growing at one to one and a half percent a year. This, combined with increasing Brazilian production and the entry of Vietnam into the market, has resulted in more coffee being produced and more lower quality coffee being traded. On top of this, roasters have moved from specialty arabica beans to lower-quality robusta beans.

The price of coffee has fallen to a 30-year low and the long-term prospects aren't good. Oxfam estimates that current prices reflect only 60 percent of the cost of production. Desperate farmers in Peru, Colombia and Bolivia are abandoning coffee and turning to crops like coca, the raw material for cocaine. In Ethiopia, where 700,000 households depend on coffee for their livelihoods and millions more for partial income, the decline in coffee export earnings has crippled the country's efforts to deal with the HIV/AIDS crisis.

Thirty percent of the coffee pickers in Kenya are children — giving new meaning to the phrase "small farmers."
— Mugged: Poverty in Your Coffee Cup, *Oxfam International 2002*

Seventy percent of coffee is grown by peasants on small farms. These farmers used to be able to feed their families, send their kids to school, and live in decent housing. Because of the international financial stability, coffee-producing regions were less prone to political violence. All that has changed.

Even if you don't care about the small farmers that are selling coffee beans for much less than they cost to produce, you should be concerned about the quality of the coffee. Coffee has traditionally been harvested with stringent quality controls but as prices have plunged, increased mechanization and the use of more agrochemicals has decreased the quality and increased environmental degradation in very sensitive habitats.

To put this in context, the big four coffee roasters — Kraft, Nestle, Procter & Gamble, and Sara Lee — each generate more than US$1 billion in sales from coffee, and profit margins are high. Oxfam estimates that the price for a package of ground coffee in the US is almost 4,000 percent higher than the price paid to Ugandan coffee farmers.[2]

BEING PART OF THE SOLUTION!

In April 2003, Dunkin' Donuts announced it would become the first national brand to market espresso coffees made exclusively with Fair Trade Certified coffee. Every espresso, latte, or cappuccino bought from Dunkin' Donuts will be brewed with beans certified by TransFair USA, the only independent certifier of Fair Trade products in the US.

By 2004, Dunkin' Donuts will be selling Fair Trade espresso drinks in 3100 stores across the USA. Dunkin' projects that two percent of its coffee purchases will be from Fair Trade farmers as a result of this initiative. As one of the largest retailers of coffee in the world, two percent of their purchases equates to about 1.2 million pounds (540,000 kilograms) of Fair Trade beans a year. Fair Trade coffee guarantees a price of $1.26 per pound for coffee growers. The current futures price for coffee has been hovering around 60 cents a pound.

Dunkin' Donuts Fair Trade initiative will not only bring fair prices to desperate coffee farmers, but it will also ensure a higher quality of coffee for consumers. "Our philosophy has always been to make high quality coffee accessible to as many people as possible," said Ken Kimmel, vice president of Dunkin' Donuts Concepts. "Driving demand for quality helps farmers, and Dunkin' Donuts sell 2.5 million cups of quality coffee per day. Buying Fair Trade coffee for espresso beverages is another step we can take to strengthen relationships with the farmers who grow our coffee."

Rob Stephen, Dunkin' Donuts' coffee product development manager and a board member of the Specialty Coffee Association of America, added, "Working with Fair Trade cooperatives in Central and South America will give us the opportunity to do what we do best — forge great relationships and deliver great coffee to our customers. This is important work and we look forward to doing it."

Paul Rice, CEO and president of TransFair USA, called the Dunkin' Donuts announcement "a major step forward for efforts to help coffee farmers and to protect quality coffee supplies for the years to come. It's critical that key industry retailers embrace the Fair Trade model and acknowledge the important role they can play to help solve the current crisis of low prices driving coffee farmers out of business. Dunkin' Donuts is setting an excellent industry example with this move."

Although the details may change, the story is the same whenever local industry is adversely affected by globalization. Problems arise as a result of developments such as the liberalization of previously regulated international markets; the increasing importance of financial centers such as London and New York; the huge gap between international trade in financial instruments and actual trade in real goods and services; the increased volatility of financial markets and the associated human consequences. Changes are also due to the role of major multinational corporations who are benefiting from the low prices for their raw inputs but who are also concerned about the long-term sustainability of their suppliers and the risk to their brands.

The problem inherent in globalization isn't that bad guys are out to get us. If that were the case, it would be much easier to understand and solve. The problem is that the economic structures that have emerged and their environmental and human consequences have outrun our capacity to govern them. A major theme in this book is how individuals — through their consumption or philanthropy or investment choices — can help exert a moderating influence on these market forces.

These efforts and initiatives are everywhere and are growing. Individuals, nongovernmental organizations (NGOs), governments, and progressive corporations are seeking solutions. Some of the major institutions on the international level that reflect this shift in attitude are as follows:

World Social Forum

The 2003 World Social Forum was dedicated to debating and discussing concrete strategies and alternatives to current corporate economic globalization. The forum, seeking to build alliances between social movements, unions, and NGOs, was first held at Porto Alegre, Brazil, in 2001. Built on the slogan "Another World is Possible," it attracted 20,000 people representing over 500 national and international organizations from more than 100 countries. The second annual event, held in January and February 2002, saw some 55,000 people from 131 countries. And in 2003, the forum attracted 100,000 participants representing 5,500 organizations from 126 different countries.

World Business Council for Sustainable Development

The World Business Council for Sustainable Development brings together global companies reacting to world attitudes about businesses and their responsibilities. The council is made up of 165 international companies that, for the most part, are trying to protect their own interests. But the existence of the council does show that it is serious about making changes in the way that multinational corporations operate. The companies are united by a shared interest in sustainable development through economic growth, ecological balance and social progress. Let's hope this signals a transition from greenwashing to offering real contributions to the sustainability debate.

World Economic Forum

The theme of the 2003 World Economic Forum (WEF) was "building trust," in recognition of the growing global displeasure with the agenda of the world's economic leaders and with the corporate scandals in the US. In the past, the WEF was rarely concerned with matters not directly related to world trade (at least not related in their view). Today this exclusive group of world leaders and businessmen is making efforts to look as if they are listening to the concerns that citizens of the world have in regard to sustainability and social justice issues.

At the same summit, the World Economic Forum launched an ambitious initiative to monitor the worldwide progress toward a more sustainable future. The Global Governance Initiative will assess the efforts of governments, businesses, civil society and intergovernmental organizations to meet the lofty goals set forth in the United Nations Millennium Declaration. Among the goals of the Millennium Declaration are:

- To halve the number of people living in poverty by 2015.
- To insure universal primary education by 2015.
- To halt and reverse the spread of HIV/AIDS and other major diseases by 2015.
- To fulfill commitments to reduce greenhouse gas emissions and to implement conventions related to the conservation of biodiversity.
- To halve the number of people suffering from hunger by 2015.

- To uphold the Universal Declaration of Human Rights and other agreements related to the rights of women and migrants, and ensure media freedom and the public's right to access to information.
- To insure the implementation of arms control and disarmament treaties, and strengthen the role of the United Nations in maintaining peace and security.

The initiative will consist of seven international groups of experts, each dedicated to assessing the progress and cooperation in one of the above areas. They will table a report by the 2004 annual meeting that will provide a numerical score of progress and effort made, and will also discuss the challenges and problems impeding the achievement of the goals.

In his opening speech to the 2003 World Economic Forum, Pascal Couchepin, the president of the Swiss Confederation, described the corporate shift necessary to achieve the forum's goals:

> In order to achieve this, business must once again see itself as being more than a part and servant of society. It should not focus on maximizing profits in the short-term, but rather on optimizing them in the long-term. That requires managers with skills in leadership and a feeling for social responsibility, whose performance is measured against the company's long-term success. That requires approachable, morally principled senior management who do not shy away from making commitments for the common good, for instance practice "good citizenship" and be visible to the public.[3]

G8 Summit

At the 2003 G8 summit in Evian, France, one of three major themes was enhancing sustainable development, along with promoting worldwide growth and improving security. For the first time in the history of the summit talks, a key focus was the development of strategies to achieve sustainable development in countries with the strongest economies. Although no concrete accords or binding agreements were created, the summit did bring the G8 leaders together to discuss and form action plans around social policy issues such as debt relief, poverty and hunger relief, access to clean water, developing new eco-friendly technologies, illegal logging, and conservation of marine resources.

A G8 action plan was drafted on the use of science and technology for sustainable development, recognizing the need to actively encourage and support the creation of cleaner, sustainable, and more efficient technologies. The action plan focuses on three main opportunities: cleaner, sustainable, and more efficient energy use; coordination of global observation strategies and improvement of agricultural sustainability and productivity; as well as biodiversity conservation. The action plan discusses increasing the support for alternative sources of energy and fuel, utilizing modern technologies to combat illegal logging, and promoting sustainable forest management, as well as numerous other sustainability issues.

It's heartening to know that a global conversation on corporate social responsibility is emerging. But there's vociferous disagreement on what corporate social responsibility means and how individual companies are performing. Civil society groups have justifiably criticized many of these initiatives for using soft persuasion to improve corporate performance. We've heard it all before. Remember the Kyoto Protocol? The state of corporate sustainability reporting reminds us that we can't expect corporations to stay on track without significant pressure from shareholders and other stakeholders.

TRUST US — THE STORY OF CORPORATE REPORTING

Trust Us, a global survey of corporate reporting published in 2002, was created by SustainAbility for the United Nations Environment Program. The survey provides an international benchmark for corporate reporting which reveals some interesting and some disturbing trends.

Corporate environmental reporting was spawned in the early nineties in response to a number of major incidents that placed corporations in the environmental spotlight. The earliest corporate reporters were engaging in damage control in order to gain back lost trust. Corporate reporting has evolved to the point where companies compete with each other to produce the most innovative and responsible reports. The number of companies producing reports has gone from a couple of dozen a decade ago to a few thousand today. The growth of reports that have been externally verified has grown from just four percent of the reports in their 1994 survey to 68 percent in 2002.

The *Trust Us* survey noted that the average page-length of printed reports has increased 45 percent between 2000 and 2002 — "with no associated increase in overall report quality." Through this practice, labeled the "Carpet Bombing Syndrome," companies are apparently trying to substitute quantity for quality.

In general, the authors of the *Trust Us* survey note that report quality has hit a plateau, with report scores showing negligible change since 2000. The good news is that social issues are becoming much more prevalent in company reports: reporting on social issues increasing by 24 percent. The bad news is that environmental reporting is decreasing by a rate of nine percent.

As trust in capitalism and in companies has hit new lows, corporate social responsibility (CSR) and sustainability reporting potentially offers real opportunities for companies to rebuild that trust.
— Trust Us: Global Reporters Survey of Corporate Sustainability Reporting[4]

Started in 1997 by the Coalition for Environmentally Responsible Economies (CERES), the Global Reporting Initiative (GRI) has a mission to develop and disseminate guidelines for reporting on sustainability, intended for voluntary use by organizations. The GRI became independent of CERES in 2002 and is now officially a collaborating center of the United Nations Environment Program (UNEP), working in cooperation with the UN's Global Compact.

The guidelines of the Global Reporting Initiative were first established in 2002. Sixty percent of the top 50 reports in the *Trust Us* survey used the GRI guidelines, and these companies scored, on average, eight percent higher than companies that didn't use the GRI guidelines.

Corporate reporting is evolving in part due to an increase in regulations from governments hoping to push companies towards accountability. For instance, in 2002 France announced that all companies listed on the French stock exchange must include a range of social, environmental, and labor information in their annual reports.

Energy companies have a strong showing in the report, as do other companies whose business involves direct and significant environmental impacts. Those companies that have major risk profiles have been the most active in producing reports — a sign that they are beginning to recognize the direct link between triple bottom line reporting and the sustainability of their businesses.

But there are concerns about the direction of corporate reporting. There is a growing gap between the leading minority of corporate leaders and the "silent majority." There are some 50,000 multinational companies in operation and only a very small percentage of these companies are filing relevant reports. And there is still a disconnect between reporting and performance. Companies are becoming more transparent about their actions, but not necessarily integrating sustainability concerns into their decision-making. It's still up to society to hold companies accountable for their behavior.

Where do we go from here?

We all know that social and environmental issues can hamstring companies by imposing direct liabilities that damage their reputation and suck up management's time and focus. Globalization only enhances these challenges. Problems in one part of the world can affect a company's reputation at home. And companies are often operating in difficult political environments where standards are not the same as they are at home. Another result of globalization has been that companies have outsourced more and more of their operations as they search for production advantages overseas. This has exposed them to supply chain risks that were never anticipated. Finally, globalization of the marketplace has been accompanied by globalization of the concerns and organizational capacity of civil society and social movements. That means that environmentalists and human rights groups can mobilize pressure on a world scale to counteract perceived lapses in corporate responsibility.

But the single biggest challenge to responsible globalization is an antiquated bookkeeping system. And I don't mean the outright illegal accounting of the Enrons and WorldComs. I mean a system that doesn't integrate human rights — such as access to clean air, water, food, and human decency — into the bottom line.

Traditional accounting theory only accounts for economic capital. But this completely ignores the fact that companies could not exist without human and natural capital as well. Natural resources — such as raw materials, plants, animals, and clean air — are integral to the operations of all companies. And companies would be unable to function without the human capital of their employees and customers, as well as the day-to-day infrastructure provided by local communities such as roads, drinking water, education, hospitals, and governments. Triple bottom line accounting is an attempt to gauge the real value a corporation is providing to society, not just the dollars and cents.

Defining economic, social, and environmental costs is often referred to as full-cost accounting. While the triple bottom line can list the pros and cons of company's business in regards to each of the three categories, full-cost accounting is an attempt to deliver a single number in dollars that represents all of the potential costs and benefits. For instance, if the energy industry were to embrace full-cost accounting that included the environmental cost of different types of energy, the cost of sustainable energies such as wind or solar power would suddenly become very competitive with traditional energy sources.

The European Commission's Fifth Action Program calls on the accounting profession to develop full-cost accounting so that "the consumption and use of environmental resources are accounted for as part of the full cost of production and reflected in market prices."

Let's not hold our breath waiting for the accounting profession to drive this initiative. If we want to change the world, we have to aggressively pursue positive strategies and aggressively reward positive outcomes. That's why the viewpoint of the investor or the consumer is so important. It's up to us to hold companies accountable for the full range of their costs, and to reward them to the full extent of the benefits they provide.

HOW MUCH CAN THE PLANET AFFORD?

In his latest book, *Plan B: Rescuing a Planet Under Stress and a Civilization in Trouble,*[5] Lester Brown paints a bleak picture of our progress to date:

We are cutting trees faster than they can regenerate, overgrazing rangelands and converting them into deserts, overpumping aquifers, and draining rivers dry. On our cropland, soil erosion exceeds new soil formation, slowly depriving the soil of its inherent fertility. We are taking fish from the ocean faster than they can reproduce.

We are releasing carbon dioxide (CO_2) into the atmosphere faster than nature can absorb it, creating a greenhouse effect. As atmospheric CO_2 levels rise, so does the Earth's temperature. Habitat destruction and climate change are destroying plant and animal species far faster than new species can evolve, launching the first mass extinction since the one that eradicated the dinosaurs 65 million years ago.

Throughout history, humans have lived on the Earth's sustainable yield — the interest from its natural endowment. But now we are consuming the endowment itself. In ecology, as in economics, we can consume principal along with interest in the short run, but in the long run it leads to bankruptcy.[6]

Obviously, we must change or we won't survive. Is the marketplace a viable forum for effecting this change? The dominance of corporations in our lives means that it has to be. But we can also help effect change by investing in our communities through community investing or social change philanthropy. We all need to be social investors. *Social* alludes to the interdependence of human beings living together in communities. So when we put our money to work — as investors, as consumers, as workers, as communities and as philanthropists — we must ensure that our return is in social as well as financial capital. We must make global profit in the context of global justice a reality.

Social Impact Investing: From Feeling Good to Doing Good

Business is business! And business must grow
Regardless of crummies in tummies, you know.
— *The Lorax*, Dr. Seuss

CONNECTING THE DOTS BETWEEN our investments and social change is a big stretch for most of us. So-called "ethical investments" haven't always lived up to their claims to be purer than "non-ethical" investments. And the connection between investment screening and environmental sustainability and social justice seems elusive at best. So what's a person to do?

If you've thought about this at all, you've probably started channeling your hard-earned money away from business activities you can't support and toward business activities that you can. You've taken care of your financial destiny while harmonizing your pocketbook with your concerns for society. But how do you move from the "feel good" to the "do good"?

Historically, for most social investors, it has been all about screening — because we all want to feel good about our investments. We want to sleep at night knowing that we aren't contributing to the problem. I've heard hundreds of investors say, "I don't want to own the banks or the resource companies in my portfolio." But investing in a company or mutual fund that's perfect, if it exists, won't solve our problems. You can stick your head in the sand forever but you'll be lying in the middle of a toxic waste dump when you take it out — unless we find a way to lessen the impact of our presence on this planet. The world has become a complicated place and that means that we need complex solutions. It's easy to blame multinational corporations for all of the ills of society. But until we stop driving cars and using appliances and energy and so on, we have to accept our complicity in the problems and our responsibility for the solutions.

For hundreds of years, religious investors have avoided investing in businesses that profit from products designed to kill their fellow human beings. The "sin" stocks — alcohol, tobacco, and military.

Modern social investing isn't all about sin. It has its roots in the '60s. In 1962 Rachel Carson wrote *Silent Spring* and a whole generation became concerned about corporate environmental performance. Civil rights, women's liberation, and labor rights made us increasingly aware of social justice issues around the world. During the Vietnam War, thousands of Americans divested their shares in companies that were part of the war machine. And in the late '70s international attention focused on apartheid: social investors sponsored shareholder resolutions urging companies to withdraw from South Africa. Long before Ralph Nader rained on Al Gore's parade, he began a consumer campaign against General Motors that led to the first effective shareholder campaign on product safety and hiring. Subsequent decades have brought us Bhopal, Exxon Valdez and human rights abuses in countries such as Burma, Nigeria, and the Sudan.

Since the late '90s, social investing has gone from strength to strength as more and more investors have recognized that we can have an impact. It's about sending a message. By choosing social investing you tell multinational corporations and financial markets that the world is changing: a healthy environment and common human dignity are not legitimate costs of doing business. They are the cornerstones of a strong and sustainable global economy. Our challenge as investors is to incorporate those basic human needs into a framework designed for the maximization of profit.

LEAP OF FAITH: THE ETHICAL GROWTH FUND

Canada's first socially screened mutual fund, The Ethical Growth Fund, was launched in 1986. David Levi, a former director and chair of VanCity, Canada's largest credit union, described the process:

"The first discussions around creating an ethically screened fund were an outgrowth of VanCity's desire to provide more options for its members. The creation of the Ethical Growth Fund was a unique experience because as Canada's first ethically-screened fund, there weren't any models for us to use. So a group of directors sat around one evening and came up with at least 20 potential screens. Then we went through the process of narrowing them down to the ones that we believed would be the commonly held views of our potential investors. Because we were the first, we knew the fund would be under incredible scrutiny and decided to place only black and white screens on the portfolio — e.g., if a company had a single employee in South Africa, they were out of the portfolio. Other screens like environmental performance were added after we had established our credibility. The establishment of the Ethical Growth Fund led to a complete review of VanCity's practices to ensure the credit union itself would qualify to be in its own fund."

To address this need, social investing is evolving from negative screening (avoiding "bad companies") to solution-oriented engagement with companies — and from an exclusive focus on moral values (my values and your values vis-à-vis our investments) to looking at corporate accountability in the context of risk to long-term shareholder and stakeholder value. Globalization has created a whole new set of liabilities for companies and it's our responsibility as shareholders to preserve that value for future generations.

In my experience as an advisor and now as CEO and portfolio manager of Real Assets Investment Management, I have found that the bell curve is a useful way to describe the social, environmental, and ethical performance of the companies in an index such as the

Standard and Poor's 500. About 20 percent of the companies are really bad actors and a similar number are pretty decent corporate citizens. The rest fall in the gray area in the middle: they do some things well and some things badly.

The Real Assets Social Leaders Fund is a fund that focuses on the best of the best in the leading 20 percent. The Real Assets Social Impact Fund focuses on driving the companies in the middle to become more like the top 20 percent.

Figure 2.1: Social Impact Investing at Real Assets

Credit: Prepared by Real Assets Investment Management using proprietary information.

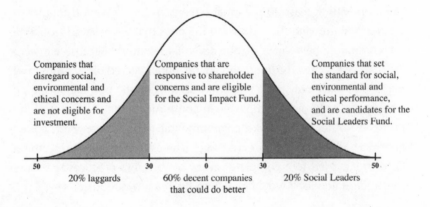

| Companies that disregard social, environmental and ethical concerns and are not eligible for investment. | Companies that are responsive to shareholder concerns and are eligible for the Social Impact Fund. | Companies that set the standard for social, environmental and ethical performance, and are candidates for the Social Leaders Fund. |

50   30   0   30   50

20% laggards   60% decent companies   20% Social Leaders
                    that could do better

REAL ASSETS SOCIAL LEADERS FUND

Great companies doing great things! The 25 to 50 companies in this global equity fund are committed to social and environmental leadership through progressive practices and cutting-edge products and services. We expect them to demonstrate the financial benefits of leadership in those areas!

REAL ASSETS SOCIAL IMPACT FUND

Making good companies even better! Proactive shareholder strategies make an impact on the companies held in this conservative balanced fund. Pushing companies to improve social and environmental performance means better long-term value for shareholders.

It isn't enough to separate the good companies from the bad companies. If we just concentrate on screening out the bad ones, they might try a little harder to obey the laws of the land — but then the companies that already meet our screening criteria, the companies in the gray area, will just continue to do business as usual. And business as usual just isn't good enough anymore. We need to focus on the good companies in our portfolios and encourage them to become even better companies. In so doing, we'll raise the bar for everyone and the laggards will have to improve their practices just as a rising tide raises all ships. So we screen out the worst, highlight the best, and shift the *entire* curve to the right through shareholder action.

I don't mean to imply that screening doesn't have a role — it does. Companies vary widely in their ability to handle social, environmental, and ethical risks. So screening does give you an edge by reducing some of the company-specific risk in your portfolio. It's just more due diligence. Screening is part and parcel of shareholder activism. We need to be able to exclude companies that have shown themselves incapable of addressing fundamental issues in a constructive and effective way. And we need to have a way of ending conversations with companies that ignore our concerns.

ESTABLISHING BENCHMARKS

When Amy Domini was working as a stockbroker in 1980, some of her clients questioned whether it was possible to align their investments with their values. She realized that they needed a benchmark to determine whether there was a cost or a benefit to being a socially responsible investor. The problem was there was no entity undertaking comprehensive and systematic analysis of the social and environmental performance of US corporations.

So, in 1988, Amy, along with her partners Peter Kinder and Steve Lydenberg, launched Kinder, Lydenberg, Domini & Co. (KLD) The launch of the Domini 400 Social IndexSM (DSI) — an index of 400 primarily large-capitalization US corporations which were selected based on a wide range of social and environmental criteria — soon followed. Today, KLD Research & Analytics Inc. supplies social investment research, benchmarks, compliance, and consulting services to leading investment institutions worldwide, in addition to supporting the DSI.

In the early 1990s in Canada, the socially responsible investment (SRI) movement consisted of a small number of mutual funds struggling to establish market share. In response to the desire for up-to-date, objective, and comprehensive social and environmental research, Michael Jantzi launched Michael Jantzi Research Associates Inc. (MJRA).The creation of the Canadian Social Investment DatabaseTM, and MJRA's best-of-sector research methodology, allowed social investors for the first time to systematically integrate these issues into their portfolios.

Today MJRA provides a full range of social investment research and support services to institutional clients and financial professionals who integrate social and environmental criteria into their investment decisions. In addition to undertaking social research and analysis, MJRA works with its clients to define screening criteria and proxy voting guidelines, and supports the Jantzi Social Index® (JSI), a market capitalization-weighted common stock index consisting of 60 Canadian companies that pass a set of broadly-based social and environmental screens.

Fortunately, when we recognized that screening out bad companies wasn't as powerful a lever for improving corporate behavior as we thought it would be, new role models emerged, such as the California Public Employees Retirement System (CalPERS) and the New York City Employees Retirement System (NYCERS). These large US public pension plans became very active shareholders who began to make a difference both financially and socially. The rest of us started to wake up to the possibility of reducing both social and financial liabilities and of increasing shareholder value through shareholder activism.

Investors — large and small, individual and institutional — were discovering that, acting together, we could use our influence as shareholders to build a better future for us all — and that we wouldn't have to sacrifice our vision for a just society in order to achieve competitive financial returns. There's mounting evidence that social investing doesn't have to come at the cost of performance — empirical evidence that shows a positive link between companies that are socially responsible and strong financial performers. The studies of studies are a good place to start.

A study by Orlitzky, Schmidt, and Rynes in 2002 was a thorough analysis of 52 previous studies that accounted for a whopping 33,878 observations on the link between corporate social responsibility (CSR) and financial performance. Their conclusion was that there is a positive link between a company's corporate virtue (in the form of social and environmental responsibility), and the financial performance of the company. In other words, companies that do good, perform better.[1]

Harvard and University of Michigan scholars Margolis and Walsh performed an extensive analysis of the literature in 2001, analyzing 95 studies on the link between corporate social and environmental responsibility and financial performance. They found that the majority of studies pointed to a positive correlation between the CSR of a company and its financial performance. At the very least, the authors concluded that there was no evidence of any negative effect to firms practicing and promoting social and environmental responsibility.[2]

A 1999 study by Roman, Hayibor, and Agle published in the journal *Business and Society* was another extensive analysis of the literature.[3] This time, 51 studies were analyzed and categorized into positive, negative, and inconclusive in regards to the link between the CSR of a company and its bottom line. Their findings were emphatic: 33 studies showed a positive correlation, 14 produced inconclusive results, and only five showed a negative relationship.

An earlier study by Jeff Frooman took a different tack in approaching the question of CSR and company profitability: he wanted to uncover whether or not socially irresponsible actions by a company had a negative effect on the company's stock price. In his analysis of 27 event studies in which socially irresponsible or illegal behavior occurred (e.g., oil spills, antitrust suits, pollution), he found strong evidence that the misbehavior of a company had a strong effect on the value of the company. Those companies that engage in socially irresponsible actions — and get caught — suffer from an immediate and permanent loss of share-holder wealth. He concluded that all things being equal, CSR is a necessary requirement for the financial success and longevity of a company.[4]

Between 1950 and 1990, companies with an ethical reputation grew 11.3 percent compared with the Dow Jones Index growth of 6.3 percent.
— Kenneth Labich, Fortune magazine[5]

Some studies have compared companies recognized as socially responsible with traditional lists of top economic performers to see how they match up. Verschoor and Murphy's 2002 study looked to compare the financial accomplishments of the companies in *Business Ethics'* list of the 100 Best Corporate Citizens against the remaining companies in Standard and Poor's 500 (a traditional list of the top economic performers in the corporate world). The authors found that the companies in the 100 Best Corporate Citizens list outperformed the rest of the companies in the S & P 500 by over ten percent. Even more impressive, they found that the Mean Market Value Added of the 100 Best Corporate Citizens (difference between what shareholders could get from cashing in their stocks now to what they put in originally), was more than four times that of the remaining companies — a difference of $28 billion.[6]

VALUE ADDED:
THE REWARDS OF SOCIAL RESPONSIBILITY

The Dow Jones Sustainability Group Index (DJSGI) is a creation of the Dow Jones Index and Sustainable Asset Management (SAM). The DJSGI represents the top ten percent of the leading sustainability companies in the world and represents over 300 companies. According to Benefits Canada, between 1994 and August of 2002 the DJSGI outperformed the

Dow Jones Global Index (DJGI) by approximately 40 percent.[7] SAM calculated similar results for the index, estimating that the sustainable index posted a 50 percent higher return between 1994 and the beginning of 2001.[8]

The Domini Social Index (DSI) was one of the first socially responsible indexes created. The DSI has outperformed the S&P 500 on a total return basis and on a risk-adjusted basis since its inception in 1990. As of March 2003, the ten year annualized return on investment for the DSI was 9.13 percent, compared to 8.54 percent for the S&P 500.[9]

The Jantzi Social Index® (JSI) consists of 60 Canadian companies that pass a number of social and environmental screens and is modeled on the Standard and Poor/Toronto Stock Exchange 60. From its inception in 2000 through to May of 2003, the JSI outperformed the Standard and Poor's 60 by over six percent, the Standard and Poor's/Toronto Stock Exchange Composite by over three percent, and the Dow Jones Canada 40 by almost 14 percent.[10]

It only stands to reason that these results manifest themselves in competitive financial returns for socially responsible investment products. Lipper Inc. and Morningstar are well-respected tracking firms that produce rankings of mutual funds based on their performance. Of the 51 screened funds tracked by the Social Investment Forum, nearly two-thirds (65 percent) earned one of the two highest rankings for performance from Lipper and/or Morningstar in 2002. This compares to 63 percent of all such funds getting top marks. Of the 18 socially responsible funds with over $100 million in assets, 72 percent received top marks from one or both of the tracking firms. A total of 43 percent of the screened funds tracked by the Forum received four or five stars from Morningstar versus 32.5 percent of the general mutual fund universe. According to Lipper, socially responsible funds grew in 2002 while the rest of the industry contracted. And socially responsible funds experienced net inflows of $1.5 billion, while US diversified equity funds saw outflows of nearly $10.5 billion.[11]

According to Tim Smith, president of the Social Investment Forum:

During 2002, the country faced pending war, countless corporate scandals and a slumping stock market. Nonetheless, socially and environmentally responsible funds continued to receive high marks from the leading tracking agencies. This is persuasive proof that investing in companies with good social and environmental track records is consistent with financial performance. As a result, we can say categorically that socially responsible funds can go toe to toe with the broad universe of mutual funds and, in fact, do better than other types of funds.[12]

Alisa Gravitz, the executive director of Co-op America, a non-profit investor education organization, thinks that the recent wave of corporate scandals is driving investor concern:

We're seeing more and more investors concerned about the companies in which they invest. They're more active investors who demand that companies have ethical financial, social and environmental practices. Active involvement in shareholder advocacy has gone through the roof over the past few years. Socially responsible investing provides the best way for investors to demand better financial and ethical performance from companies.[13]

The financial world has apparently noticed the link between CSR and profitability too, according to a couple of recent surveys. A survey by PricewaterhouseCoopers asked 1,161 CEOs from 33 countries about their opinions on CSR. Seventy percent of them stated that corporate social responsibility is vital to the profitability of any company.[14] A 2001 poll of global opinion leaders performed for the Prince of Wales Business Leaders Forum tells us that 76 percent of those polled agreed that the degree to which a firm is seen as corporately responsible will affect share price in the future. Forty-two percent agreed strongly with this statement.[15]

WHERE DO YOU START?

Find an investment advisor who can give you information and advice about social impact investing. When I became an investment professional, there was only a handful of people in the industry that could provide this advice to their clients. That number has grown. You can find an advisor who will help you incorporate concerns for society and financial needs. The Social Investment Organization in Canada and the Social Investment Forum in the US provide lists of their professional members on their websites.

STEPHEN WHIPP: A PIONEER IN SOCIAL INVESTING

Stephen is a financial planner at Berkshire Investment Group in Victoria, British Columbia. He's a baby boomer and, like many of his generation, he did his share of protest marching during the '70s. Like many pioneers, Stephen has come to social impact investing because of his personal values. I interviewed him in 2003 to find out what motivated him to specialize in social investing:

"As a journalist in Northern British Columbia in the 1970s, I became aware of how decisions affecting resource sustainability, aboriginal land claims, and basic human rights were made. I saw a lot of things that just weren't right. I could see that governments and corporations were not acting within a set of values based on the long-term good of society and the natural environment. Since then, I have been lucky to work in a number of fields — public legal education, land claim negotiations, communications, environmental research, political activism, and now financial planning. In each, I have witnessed the inability of people to have a real impact on democracy and capitalism. Politicians and corporations work on cycles of five years or less with an eye on the next election or quarterly earnings report, not the long-term impact of their behavior. Meanwhile, Mother Nature operates on cycles that are decades or centuries in length.

As resources — such as wood, water, and even the ozone — get more and more depleted and as companies seek out cheap labor in developing countries, I believe that it is the responsibility of those of us in the more developed parts of the world to ensure that we are not condoning irresponsible, short-sighted corporate behavior that is only concerned about today's profits.

That's why I've specialized in social investing. Many of my clients share my concerns and values and are passionate about social investing. Social investing isn't just about doing the right thing. It's also about sustainable business models. Companies are being forced to consider possible future environmental or work force liabilities or costs as scandals start to jump up and bite them. It's no longer seen as a fringe or politically driven investment strategy.

I'm really excited about the impact that shareholder activism is having on corporate behavior at home and abroad. I can get my clients excited about this. They're not satisfied with just the "clean hands" approach anymore. Sure, they like owning good companies that have a sustainable business model but they also want to know that they're making a difference and that means owning companies that can change, companies that can raise the bar for others in their sector.

And it's up to us as investors to hold their feet to the fire. Just as governments and corporations must be accountable for the impact of their behavior on people and the planet, we need to be responsible for the impact of our investments. Otherwise, we wasted a lot of time protesting."

A growing number of investment companies and financial professionals have turned away from traditional investing, with its singular goal of maximizing profit, towards the tenets of social investing. In Canada, the Social Investment Organization has been promoting social investing since 1989 and now boasts over 500 members, representing the financial investments of over 200,000 Canadians. Organizations such as Social Investment Organization and Social Investment Forum are providing the support and organization that the social investment community needs in order to grow to a point where it becomes the norm and not the exception in investment circles. From organizing conferences to sharing best practices to teaching the how-tos of shareholder advocacy, these organizations are committed to increasing the market share of social investing while also ensuring that members maximize the efficacy of their investment decisions.

SUCHETA RAJAGOPAL:
A SOCIAL AND INVESTMENT ACTIVIST

Sucheta Rajagopal has been an active member of the social investment community for some time. We chatted about how she has integrated her concerns for society with her investment practice. Currently a vice-president and investment advisor at Hampton Securities in Toronto, Sucheta provides social investment advice to all of her clients. She has always been interested in the influence that corporate behavior has on our lives:

"If we don't fight for better corporate behavior, who will? I feel it's important to monitor their behavior and impel them to take their societal responsibilities more seriously. Before I joined the financial world, I used my consumer dollars to drive social change. I joined boycotts and tried to buy products of companies whose policies were more progressive. When I became an investment advisor, it made sense to use investment dollars in the same way.

Social investing fits naturally with many other things I do, such as taking public transit, buying organic foods, volunteering, and making a daily commitment to the three Rs (reduce, reuse, recycle).

Most of my clients are in their 40s, 50s, and 60s and are very concerned about the world we live in. They are particularly troubled by environmental issues and want to take action. They welcome information from me on what can be done. I give them updates on corporate behavior, shareholder resolutions, and directions on how to vote their shares.

Although they sound like a bunch of radicals, my clients are conservative with their money. They want sound low risk investments. They prefer owning larger blue chip companies and they are interested in the concept of corporate engagement as a way of making these companies more responsive to our concerns, but sometimes they're skeptical about whether we're achieving results.

The biggest concern I hear is about the banks. Without disclosure of corporate lending portfolios and practices, we are probably unwittingly supporting companies that we would never own directly. Clients and prospects also have a tough time biting the bullet on some best of sector companies (e.g., resource extraction companies). I tell them that there are no perfect companies, and we have to start somewhere if we want to raise the bar."

Membership organizations, such as the Social Investment Organization (SIO) in Canada and the Social Investment Forum (SIF) in the US and UK, are non-profit groups whose mission is to advance social investment. Membership is open to any financial professionals or organizations interested in social investing. The SIO and SIF provide members with information, research, networking, and organization services. Both organizations work to promote, develop, and advance the three aspects of social investment: positive and negative screening, community investment, and shareholder advocacy.

The Social Investment Organization and the Social Investment Forum are focused on serving their membership; however, they also provide lots of information for the individual investor. Much of the research performed by them is available to anyone. Publications, investment advice, and key indices monitoring the performance of socially responsible funds are all available on their websites. The aim of the SIO and the SIF is not to create an exclusive investment community but to expose as many investors as possible to social investing in order to effect the greatest change. For information on how to contact these and other organizations in the social investment field, see the Resources section at the end of this book.

INVESTING WITH IMPACT! SMALL CHANGES + LARGE CORPORATIONS = SIGNIFICANT CHANGE

BY PERRY ABBEY

For many years, Perry Abbey and I were the only investment advisors in Canada who focused exclusively on social investing. After analyzing the social, environmental, and ethical performance of companies, Perry uses all of the same metrics as the other investment pros, starting with fundamental analysis. A company's relative growth rate, profitability, and cash flows are all critical to determining its long-term investment potential. He even visits the arcane world of technical analysis! Which is probably not helpful long term, but it can sometimes reflect the shorter term irrationality of the market, which, at the end of the trading day is always right, even when it's wrong!

As a social impact investment advisor, I have had the great privilege to have clients that are some of the most principled

and thoughtful investors in Canada. They are at the cutting edge of
social change and clearly part of Margaret Mead's small coterie of
citizens changing the world.

This doesn't make the investment process any easier. If anything
it becomes more difficult! Investors who have deeply held personal
values have spent a lifetime applying those values to the real world
around them. So when I listen to them, and nod, and agree with
their vision of the world, and then turn around and suggest that they
invest some of their hard earned savings in a large multinational corporation or bank — it's not what they had in mind.

Deb will tell us later in this book about her vision for aggressive
roll-up-your-sleeves social impact investing in the mainstream of the
marketplace. Leveraging capital to push corporate behavior in a positive direction changes the standard for all corporations, a shareholder stick-and-carrot approach.

I want to look at another segment of the market, comprising
those companies that are already motivated to make positive change
in their operations. The premise is that large corporations who make
small changes will have a significant social or environmental impact
through the sheer size of their operations. This usually makes a positive contribution to their traditional bottom line at the same time.
Voluntary, incremental change that leads to increased profitability
doesn't need shareholder engagement to keep it going. But sometimes, shareholder or stakeholder action kickstarts the process.

CLEANING UP THE MESS: REAL ASSETS AND THE SOCIAL LEADERS FUND

If you believe that big companies have had a lot to do with messing
up this planet, it's only common sense that they will have to be part
of the clean up as well. Some will need to be prodded and pushed
into "doing the right thing" but a smaller and growing segment of
the corporate sector was either founded with such lofty goals in mind
or has evolved in this direction. Those companies that can be seen to
be leading the way to a more equitable and sustainable world are
what Real Assets have called "Social Leaders." Not at all coinciden-
tally, these are also the "feel good" companies that social investors

inevitably want to invest in. They will sleep easier knowing that they own "Great Companies Doing Great Things" (which is Real Assets' slogan to encompass the company's approach to social investment).

But what exactly is a social leader? Some may provide a particular service or technology that may be indispensable to a sustainable world. Some may be truly exemplary employers or have an overwhelming beneficial positive impact on the communities or regions they do business in. And some have no single "best practice or product" example but conduct so many different parts of their business in a superior manner that they too can be viewed as Social Leaders. But the definition is evolving so we are best to look at some examples.

Electrolux

You probably remember the old "tank" vacuum cleaners of the fifties and sixties, usually associated with a high price tag, high quality, and high durability. Yes, that would be an Electrolux! (ELUXB on the Stockholm exchange). While they are no longer in that kind of vacuum business, they are a company that we have considered a "Social Leader" for some years now.

In 1992, Electrolux faced what big companies around the world have begun to dread — a Greenpeace protest on their front lawns. Greenpeace activists dumped used refrigerators on the grounds of Electrolux headquarters in Stockholm to highlight their opinion that the company wasn't doing enough to reduce its use of ozone-depleting chlorofluorocarbons (CFCs). Electrolux's reaction to that challenge has been a defining moment in the company's history. Instead of denying the existence of a problem and hiding behind a communications strategy, they embarked on an ambitious campaign to integrate their environmental policy into all facets of their operation.

Only one year after Greenpeace was lobbing refrigerators on their doorstep, Electrolux released the first CFC-free refrigerator. From there their goal has been constant improvement. Today they are a leader in environmental reporting and have been at the forefront in pushing for corporate social responsibility. Electrolux has committed itself to exceeding the regulatory requirements for energy efficiency in their products and has supported efforts to make such regulations stricter. They have set goals to reduce the waste, pollution, and energy use associated with their manufacturing processes. In essence, they have committed to continually raising the bar for environmental achievement in their industry. Along the way they have:

- Been selected by a number of environmental investment funds.
- Produced internationally recognized annual environmental reports that are verified by third-party auditors.
- Certified the majority of their operations to ISO 14000 standards.
- Not only become CFC-free in their North American and European markets but also have made their China and Brazil markets CFC-free.
- Won numerous awards for the creation of energy and water efficient appliances.
- Created a dry-cleaning process that only uses CO_2 instead of harsh chemicals.
- Created a solar-powered lawnmower.
- Increased the efficiency of their appliance products every year since 1998.
- Increased the percentage of their profits related to green products to 20 percent.
- Created the first cooking appliance that uses induction — reducing the energy consumption by over 30 percent.
- Been an outspoken supporter of the European initiative to make individual manufacturers responsible for the disposal of their products once they've been used.

Electrolux's motivation to change their model of conducting business originated in large part as a response to stakeholder action. There are no perfect companies. It is this realization that makes it a difficult task to identify companies such as Electrolux and defend the decision to call them social leaders. Regardless, when Real Assets launched its Social Leaders Fund in March 2002, Electrolux seemed like an obvious choice.

The fund also included Whole Foods Markets (WFMI on Nasdaq), in the portfolio from inception. Whole Foods is a terrific company in many ways. It sells responsibly grown, organic, and Fair Traded foodstuffs to an aging and increasingly health-conscious America. But the management at Whole Foods has a decidedly anti-union philosophy, and recently, an attempt at limited union certification was met with hostility on the part of the company.

No one has ever described me as a strident unionist — but I do recognize that unions have been of inestimable value in the history of the struggle for social justice in North America. As social investors, we would expect a Social Leader to find common ground, not battle ground, when facing this type of development in their corporate history. So what to do? Was Whole Foods still truly a Social Leader? Real Assets didn't think so, and out it went. Not the typical investment committee decision for what was a very profitable position in the fund — but this is a fund that is cutting new ground in the investment world.

Seeking out "great companies doing great things" in the social, ethical, and environmental sense is not an approach common in the investment business today. While the industry is awash with examples of due diligence being done for purely financial attributes, social and environmental responsibility has seldom been considered at the very onset of the process. The active search for outstanding social and environmental performers is a break from the traditional SRI screening process as well. The task is not to screen out the "bad actors" or to find the minimally acceptable corporations, but to try to identify the very best examples of corporate behavior, including those companies that are providing the technologies or services that are needed to lead us to sustainability and social justice.

I'll get back with some more examples of what I consider to be social leaders, but first I want to acknowledge another fund, this one out of Portland Oregon, that has a similar approach.

Portfolio 21

Portfolio 21 was launched in September 1999, on the premise expressed in their literature: "In the 21st century and beyond, bold new thinking will be required to transform our society into one that is in balance with nature."

They quote Paul Hawken, author of *The Ecology of Commerce: A Declaration of Sustainability*, "The future belongs to those who understand that doing more with less is compassionate, prosperous, and enduring and thus more intelligent, even competitive."[1]

This mutual fund's emphasis on sustainability is clear from their investment selection criteria. They are looking for companies cognizant of the ecological impact of their products who are actively reducing these impacts. They favor companies that implement their capital investments in an ecologically sensitive manner, whether this takes the traditional forms of plant and equipment or works through investment in research and development of environmentally superior products or technologies. Ideally, their investees will demonstrate leadership as sustainability advocates, through the education of their related stakeholders, and through the implementation of sound environmental management systems. And of course, companies with higher resource use efficiency and low or no environmental liabilities will be sought out. In addition, as if this list of criteria isn't already a tall order for their investment managers, Portfolio 21 has set out a detailed outline of selection criteria in the emerging and very difficult area of biotechnology.

CARSTEN HENNINGSEN: THE DRIVE TO SUSTAINABILITY

Carsten Henningsen is the chair of Portfolio 21 and has a long history in social and environmental investing. In a phone interview in July 2003, Carsten commented on the challenges for the fund, noting that there simply are not enough great sustainability prospects in the US market. As a result, the fund is very much a global fund. After researching more than 2,000 companies worldwide, Portfolio 21 is currently invested in 54.

"We are still very early on the sustainability curve. As the eco-crisis worsens and the world moves from the environmental stewardship model of the 1990s to one of real environmental sustainability, concern from consumers, corporations, and governments will drive change and open up hundreds, if not thousands, of new investment candidates that meet our criteria."

In a refreshing observation, he notes that the portfolio does not remove a holding simply because they are in a cyclical downturn, unless of course their commitment to moving towards sustainability is also in question. Sounds like Warren Buffet in a green suit! He also recognizes that even for the best companies, the drive to sustainability is just beginning. As I will suggest later when looking at companies like Interface and Swiss Re (both of which are Portfolio 21 holdings), some of the most important strides a company can take are made by identifying and quantifying the problems and opportunities posed by sustainability. All that's required then is — well, hard work!

Portfolio 21. Traditional negative social screens in the background but the emphasis is on finding the positive attributes of companies dedicated to making their businesses sustainable. And as more and more companies wake up to the competitive advantage such change offers, this should be a very good portfolio to be in!

Bravo Portfolio 21! A clear choice for sustainability. Of course, many other social funds are available these days. Some are simply conventional funds with a basic screening overlay, others are more or less active on the shareholder engagement front, and some — such as alternate energy funds — are more narrowly focused. But I think the Social Leaders Fund and Portfolio 21 really exhibit the leading edge of a positive approach to investing for a better tomorrow. Over time, the growth of other complementary funds with a social impact approach may motivate more corporations to join the exclusive club represented by these funds. Let's look at a few more great companies to demonstrate what we mean by a social leader.

Birds for Baking Soda: Church and Dwight

We're all familiar with the Arm and Hammer brand name. I doubt if there are many of us who don't have a box of baking soda in the fridge or who don't add it to our laundry occasionally. Arm and Hammer is just one of the consumer brand names for the Princeton, New Jersey-based Church and Dwight Company.

Church and Dwight have been environmentally conscious since their inception in 1846. Church and Dwight's main product — sodium bicarbonate or baking soda — is an environmentally benign substance that has been used in place of chemicals and harsh detergents in a range of different cleaning processes. Perhaps because their main product is so kind to the environment, Church and Dwight have always seen good corporate social responsibility as being vital to their bottom line.

Church and Dwight is not a Johnny-come-lately to environmental stewardship. They started using recycled packaging as early as 1907, and today use over 80 percent recycled paper in all facets of their business. At the turn of the century (the 20th century, that is), Church and Dwight were issuing their famous bird cards inside of each package of Arm and Hammer Baking Soda with the logo, "For the good of all, do not destroy the birds." A deeply felt connection with nature was what inspired the early founders of the company to try to educate the public about the importance of birds. Around the time that the company was sponsoring the first Earth Day in 1970, they introduced the first phosphate-free detergent. They later prompted the detergent industry to follow their lead when they introduced concentrated cleaning formulas that required half as much packaging.

Today they continue to be an environmental leader in the world of large corporations. Their line of baking soda-based industrial cleaners eliminates the need for harsh chemicals and solvents traditionally used by industries. Of the over 300 chemicals that are regulated in the US, Church and Dwight use only four of them in their manufacturing facilities. Their corporate philosophy is wedded to the concept that environmental sustainability is crucial to the bottom line. As well, stakeholder engagement is seen as a necessary component of their daily business, thus employees, partners, and consumers are all involved with the direction of each project undertaken.

Church and Dwight have developed an incredibly strong brand image through their environmental initiatives and have been rewarded with strong consumer loyalty due to their sustainable actions.

From Laundry to Liability: Swiss Re

Here's a social leader and a sustainable pick you'll find in both Portfolio 21 and the Social Leaders funds. Swiss Re is a leading global reinsurance company operating in more than 30 countries worldwide. Reinsurance is simply the business of managing risk by spreading it over a larger number of individual direct insurers in the event of a large magnitude disaster, natural or otherwise. Events such as the 9/11 terrorist attacks, unusual floods, or earthquakes would be too costly for single insurance companies to cover. Since planning for these risks is a very big-picture, long-term endeavor, it is perhaps not surprising that a reinsurance company would be a leader in recognizing the potential costs of environmental degradation and business disruption that logically follows the effects of global warming.

Swiss Re was a leading partner with the United Nations Environment Program in launching its insurance industry initiative on sustainability in 1995. The 88 international insurance companies that signed the initiative recognize that increased social, environmental, and financial costs are inevitable if economic development is not compatible with human welfare and a healthy environment. It goes on to lay out some general principles of sustainable development as they relate to sound business management, environmental management, and communications strategies required to get the message out. All of which may be pretty obvious stuff to the reader, but not necessarily to the average corporate reader. Most telling to me is that it is coming from an industry whose core competencies — identifying and managing risk — are precisely the skill set needed to steer the planet to a better future. Any time we can get a more precise handle on the nature and magnitude of social and environmental risks, we come that much closer to identifying effective, and most likely profitable, solutions.

I won't put you to sleep with the types of day-to-day environmental liability policies that the insurance industry deals with — exciting only to an insurance salesperson, I'm sure. But I will touch on a few small innovations from Swiss Re that may illustrate their potential to effect positive change. One is simply a bonus system geared to waste disposal and manufacturing practices, where a premium bonus kicks in when long-term environmental loss claims are kept low — a win-win approach certainly, but not exactly revolutionary.

The next one is a bit more exciting and is essentially a "Disposal Policy" whereby the manufacturer pays an out-front premium in exchange for the insurer taking on the responsibility and costs involved in collecting and recycling long-lived products such as automobiles or electronic equipment. In order to be effective, this initiative will need statutory regulations such as the initiative that Electrolux and others are spearheading to make individual manufacturers responsible for the disposal of their products after use. This type of progressive insurance policy will help lead us away from our current habit of packing our landfills full of potentially recyclable, and potentially hazardous, materials.

Swiss Re also has a progressive insurance rate system that takes into consideration the positive or negative environmental impact of the client's operation. A fundamental part of the business model of all insurance companies is their underlying investment portfolios, which are critical to both their profitability and their liability reserve requirements. Swiss Re has allocated a portion of its overall portfolio to sustainability investments in both private and public opportunities since 1995.

From monitoring their air travel carbon emission impact — "as much as necessary, as little as possible" — to the organic sourcing for their 2,500 company cafeteria meals a day, Swiss Re has put significant thought into the management of their supply chain. For example, their 2002 report indicates they generated 7,778 tons (7,056.2 metric tons) of carbon emissions from their corporate air travel in 2001, or 70 percent of their total footprint. Sounds like a lot, but for a global company with 8,000 employees, identifying the impact is the first step in reducing it and they have been charting their carbon progress per employee since 1999. Incidentally, recent calculations show that the average North American's carbon emission footprint is about ten tons (9.072 metric tons) on an annual basis, not including industrial emissions.

Sustainable Sustenance: Hain Celestial

Mention of the Swiss Re cafeteria, which conjures up visions of Swiss raclette cheese drizzled over little organic "pommes vapeur," has stimulated my appetite. Because what and how we eat is so intrinsic to the human experience and strongly affects our quality of life, we must look to the food industry for some of our social leaders. And I've noticed that I get far more "buy" orders for these types of stocks just before lunch time in Vancouver!

I was born in 1952 and food was a significant part of my family's budget. Just look at the trend over the half-century (ouch) since then.

Figure 3.1: Percentage of Family Income Spent on Food

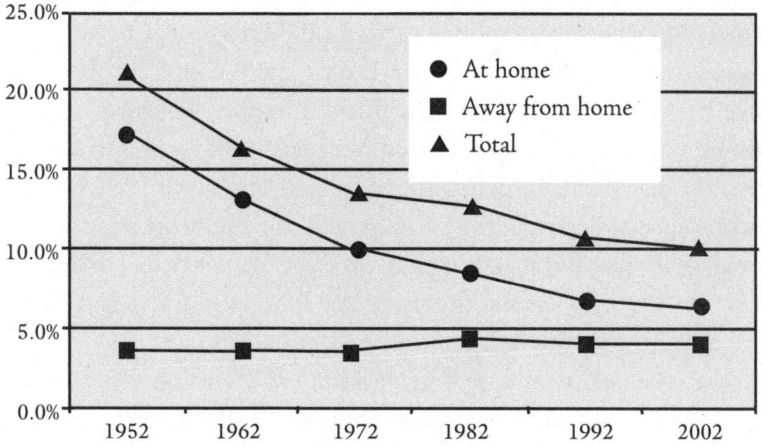

Credit: Perry Abbey. Source: US Department of Agriculture[2].

Looking at this chart you get the sense that food is getting closer and closer to being "free." At the same time an aging and increasingly health-conscious America is looking more and more for healthier, tastier food — and this demographic trend is only likely to intensify. Given the cost numbers above, there would seem to be few real inhibitors in supply and demand to a continuing sharp growth rate and market share increase in the natural and organic food sector.

Hain Celestial Group (HAIN on Nasdaq), was formed from the merger in 2000 of Hain Food Group, a leading natural, organic, and specialty food company and Celestial Seasonings, a leader in specialty teas. The company also has a strategic alliance with H.J. Heinz to produce natural and organic food. Hain's business strategy, in what is still a fairly fragmented market sector, has been one of merger and acquisition. This is always a difficult strategy, but after some initial integration problems with Celestial, they seem to be well on track as a leading and diversified supplier to the natural foods market. Currently, they have some twenty five different brands including Hain, Celestial, Health Valley, Earth's Best, Arrowhead Mills, Bearitos, Yves Veggie Cuisine, and on and on. Hain's holdings are so diverse that you've probably already had contact with this company.

Health, sustainability, and organics all go hand in hand. Currently between 50 and 60 percent of Hain's products are organically grown and as of 2002 all of these meet the new regulations of the US Department of Agriculture for the National Organic Program. The company has been a leader in advocating food production that is free of genetically modified organisms (GMO), with a corporate policy requiring non-genetically engineered ingredients for all of its all-natural and organic products. In 1999 its Earth's Best baby food brand became the first baby food brand certified GMO-free as well as certified organic.

Not available to my mother back in 1952, but oh well, too late now! Of course when I get really tired of the selection at the organic sandwich and deli in my urban office tower food court, I can always hold my nose and head for a McDonald's veggie burger supplied by (Hain's) Yves Veggie cuisine! — which is probably a staple item for Hain employees, who have access to some innovative employee benefits, including a flexcare spending account for childcare and eldercare services as well as good retirement savings matching programs and stock options.

From Low Tech Organics to Ultra High Tech: Cisco Systems

Cisco Systems is widely recognized as the backbone of the Internet. Their customers run the gamut from corporations to governments, from universities to utilities, worldwide. They provide the routers and sophisticated switching gear that has contributed to the rapid growth of the Internet. The growth of their business and their profits over the last ten years has been explosive, and even after the ravages of a capital expenditure recession and bear market of 2000–2003, this is an extremely profitable and cash-rich business which has continually increased its commanding market share, good markets and bad alike.

So what makes Cisco a social leader? There is no one area of their business conduct that we could point to and say that they are exhibiting the absolute best-practice in the world. Rather Cisco is an example of a large powerful corporation that is managing many different pieces of their business in a responsible or sustainable manner. As is typical among large corporations that have this overall approach, they find that their version of the "triple bottom line" (TBL) does add to their conventional bottom line.

Cisco's version of the triple bottom line is coined as "profits, people and presence." "Profits" are obvious (and considerable). "People" represents the mutually beneficial relationships with their customers, shareholders, and the people who "work for, with, and near us" who Cisco views as essential to their strategy. "Presence" is Cisco-speak for respecting and contributing to the well-being of local and global communities.

Coining these goals is the easy part; implementing them requires a good deal more effort — and Cisco seems to be up to the challenge. I mentioned that Cisco is a very cash-rich company — sitting on something like nine billion dollars as I write this — and they have not been shy on the philanthropic front. Cisco estimates its in-kind and cash contributions donated through its Cisco Foundation totaled 200 million dollars in the period 1997 through 2002. The focus of some of these initiatives stem from Cisco's own strengths and involve educational and e-learning programs around the world such as their least-developed countries learning program. The program aims to bring education and Internet-age job skills to participants in 33 of the 48 least-developed countries in the world today, with the aim of "preparing individuals, states, and countries to build an educated, competitive, and trained information technology work-force." In total, about 70 percent of the company's giving is educa-tion-related. Cisco partners with various other organizations such as Habitat for Humanity and the Red Cross, and has a generous matching policy for employee donations to non-profits.

THINKING OUT OF THE BOX:
PROFIT AND NONPROFIT WORKING TOGETHER

To my mind, one of Cisco's most innovative programs was born out of business necessity: when the information technology capital expenditure recession hit, Cisco faced extensive layoffs of valued employees. The Community Fellowship Program offered an option: Cisco's highly talent-ed employees could work with non-profit organizations at a greatly reduced pay scale (one third) while maintaining their employee health and stock option benefits. This was not entirely altruistic, of course, since Cisco knew that it was just a matter of time until the business cycle picked up and they would be looking for these same skilled workers again.

In April 2001, the program attracted 81 employees who went to work for 21 non-profit groups. The list of these groups is impressive, and the original pilot program was extended through to 2003 to enable the par-ticipants to complete the various projects they had taken on for groups such as Second Harvest Food Bank and Habitat for Humanity. Shortly after the program wound up, it was reported that of the participants, 34 were already back to work at Cisco as the economy was slowly coming back, and a further nine had opted to stay on with the nonprofits. A real win for the employees, for Cisco, and certainly for the communities that benefited from these talented and highly trained volunteers.

It isn't just about immensely profitable companies giving money away, however. A sustainable world needs sustainable business, and Cisco has many initiatives underway on the environmental front. On the path to achieving ISO 14000 certification (they are 60 percent of the way now), Cisco has numerous programs aimed at conservation and product design. A recent EPA Energy Star award came from a relatively simple power management program aimed at Cisco's one million computer monitors nationwide — a program that will save Cisco $625,000 annually while reducing greenhouse gas emissions by 4,375 tons (3,969 metric tons) a year. A small step, a big company, and real progress towards change. Many more steps will be required.

In this technology-driven world we are entering, environmental product design and life cycle considerations must come to the fore. Cisco Design for Environment program is based upon design and electronic waste regulations of the Environmental Protection Act, the United Nations, and the European Union. It considers the potential environmental impact of a product throughout its life cycle: how customers dispose of packaging material; the amount of power consumed during product use; and upgrading or recycling of products and parts.

One of the big problems in this age of technology is the increasing e-waste as product life cycles get shorter and shorter. The company's Surplus Product Utilization and Reclamation Program (SPUR) is aimed at addressing this problem by providing take-back programs for e-waste stemming from their products. The program extends Cisco's control over its product life, ensuring that what is in fact usable is diverted back into use and that what is left is disposed of or recycled in an environmentally sensitive manner. According to Josh Garrison, Cisco service operations manager, "Cisco product going to a landfill is bad for the environment and it's bad for the Cisco brand. Our goal is for no Cisco product to reach a landfill."[3]

Dollars and Sense: Social Banking

As a Canadian, I live within a population that loves to hates its bankers. But if we are to effect change through our investments, then we must surely include the banks. Through their lending and underwriting activities in the capital markets at home and abroad, the banks become a proxy for the social, environmental, and ethical risk inherent in the operations of those companies.

To laugh often and much,
to win the respect of intelligent people and
the affection of children,
to earn appreciation of honest critics and
endure the betrayal of false friends,
to appreciate beauty,
to find the best in others,
to leave the world a bit better,
whether by a healthy child,
a garden patch,
or a redeemed social condition;
to know even one life has breathed easier
because you have lived.
This is to have succeeded!
— ATTRIBUTED TO RALPH WALDO EMERSON

You probably wouldn't expect to see this quote in a bank's annual financial statement but that's exactly what you would find, and much more, in Wainwright Bank's 2002 Annual Report. More specifically their report opens with "Wainwright Bank remains committed to all of our stakeholders — employees, customers, and communities — who have always shared an equal place at the table alongside stockholders." When we went looking for a social leader in the financial services sector, we had to go all the way to the W section to find probably the best example in banking.

Wainwright (WAIN on the Nasdaq), was founded in 1987 as a private bank, a kind of the "boutique" approach to banking, but within a few years its cofounders, Bob Glassman and John Plukas, decided that they wanted to merge their personal beliefs with their business model. In the early 1990s the vision was just beginning to form as they decided to "contemplate a second bottom line, a noble social experiment, if you will."

The vision took form quickly. In 1991, the bank made its first community development loan — to the Pine Street Inn women's shelter for rehabilitation of the facility — which seemed to spark the interest of a new wave of socially conscious depositors. Who could foresee that doing the right thing would lead to more business? Wainwright's celebration of their first decade of socially responsible lending has come and gone, and today their vision is clearly spelled out in a mission statement that resets the bar for the banking industry.

In their mission to include all their stakeholders, Wainwright has seven main focus areas, which they address both through conventional banking initiatives such as project financing and personal banking services, and through charitable giving grants. It is their version of conventional banking that sets a standard for others to look to in these areas:

Affordable Housing

This is an obvious area for a bank and Wainwright has committed some $75 million in financing to a wide range of housing projects in the Greater Boston area — affordable low-income housing, elder housing, homeless women and children housing, rehabilitative housing, living with AIDS housing… the list goes on. Impressive when you realize that this is a small bank with a market capitalization of less than $50 million.

Health Services

The focus here has been the HIV/AIDS epidemic. Their lending and deposit activities with a number of related non-profits have also been key.

Environment

The bank's environmental policy is short and to the point. The proof is in the proverbial pudding in their actual partnerships, including The Earthwatch Institute, the Union of Concerned Scientists, the Silent Spring Institute, and many others. Operating lines of credit, building financing, and endowment investment activities are the typical services provided. Wainwright is one of a relatively small group of 70 companies who are signatories to the CERES Principles. On a consumer note, their Green Loan program nets you a one percent rate reduction for home equity loans to install solar technologies.

Homelessness and Hunger

Wainwright has provided $15 million in loans since 1991 to service providers to the homeless and hungry.

Women's issues

Wainwright's approach has been primarily education-based, helping women become financially empowered as well as establishing close banking relationships with various organizations related to women's health and rights.

Diversity

Fifty percent of the bank's officers are women, and 30 percent of the total workforce is composed of employees from visible minorities who, amongst them, speak 22 languages.

Social Activism

Lastly, but perhaps most importantly, Wainwright believes that "the management of one's financial affairs is not a morally neutral endeavor; where you invest your money, and who you buy your goods and services from can influence social conditions. If not for the power of shareholders to influence the investment policies and internal practices of the corporations they own a piece of, Nelson Mandela would probably still be imprisoned and apartheid would still exist in South Africa." Wainwright has a number of initiatives in this area, the most telling of which was their 1997 acquisition of a 30 percent stake in the Trillium Asset Management Company. You may recognize Trillium's name as a frequent filer and co-filer of social and environmental shareholder resolutions. Trillium is the oldest and largest investment management firm specializing solely in socially responsible investment with an eye to leveraging capital for real change.

The Big Banks: Small Changes With a Large Impact

But as I noted, Wainwright is just a tiny player in the international banking community, so we also went looking for social leaders of a bigger scale. While their policies will not even come close to Wainwright's example, the sheer size of their operations translates into large potential impacts for relatively small steps. Let's briefly look at two of the big ones, Royal Bank of Scotland (RBS on the London Exchange), and Union Bank of Switzerland (UBS on New York or UBSN on the Swiss exchange).

To put this in perspective, both of these banks are three orders of magnitude larger than Wainwright, or well over a thousand times the size as measured by market capitalization. So if they did even five percent as much in the direction of positive social change — well, you can do the math yourself. And the good news for Wainwright is the sheer scope of the growth opportunity should they choose to go in that direction!

The Royal Bank of Scotland Group is a holding company whose members provide banking, insurance, and financial services. Its acquisition of National Westminster Bank (NatWest) made it the seventh-largest company in the UK and the second largest bank in the UK and Europe. From a slow start, Royal Bank of Scotland has leapfrogged into a leadership position in comprehensive environmental management and reporting. They have a strong commitment to reducing social exclusion in the British financial sector and in 1999, social researchers at Henderson Investors ranked Royal Bank of Scotland as the leader in environmentally responsible lending policies.

The Royal Bank of Scotland has recently signed on to the Equator Principles — a set of voluntary guidelines for managing social and environmental issues while financing international development projects. Having reduced its own CO_2 emission by 40 percent since 1990, the bank has targeted a further five percent reduction by 2004. Much of this comes through higher standards in new or retrofitted buildings, and their own actions on this front are sure to color their credit and approval process for customers dealing with their own environmental impacts.

The Union Bank of Switzerland is one of the largest globally-integrated investment services firms and has played a pioneering role in encouraging financial institutions to accept sustainability as a business imperative. It has excellent internal environmental management systems and sets concrete achievable goals for year-over-year improvement to its in-house ecology. This Swiss bank incorporates social and environmental criteria in its lending and underwriting activities. On the underwriting side, initial due diligence is conducted by investment banking personnel. If there are indications of greater environmental risk, external environmental experts are consulted as part of the due diligence process. The credit risk process includes "financially relevant" environmental factors. In February 2002, the bank announced that it was withdrawing from the Ilisu dam project in Turkey because of social and environmental concerns. This is the first time that we've seen a financial sector firm publicly acknowledge social and environmental risks in announcing its decision to pull out of a project.

Really though, it just comes down to a willingness to acknowledge the obvious:

> A company that puts the interests of its shareholders first through good corporate governance will find its stock more attractive to investors. A bank that protects the privacy of its clients will win their trust. An asset manager who takes account of environmental criteria will attract additional assets. And a financial institution that has a strong stance in corporate responsibility will attract top talent.
> — MARCEL OSPEL, CHAIRMAN OF THE UNION BANK OF SWITZERLAND

So what is a real social leader? At Real Assets, we just say, "Great companies doing great things!" This is a new approach and still evolving, as it should. Judging from some of the examples in this and the next chapter, there is no conventional investment wisdom to classify these companies. Value? Growth? Large Cap? Small Cap? Even by conventional socially responsible investment standards, we come up with a blank. I guess we're really looking for companies that have a positive impact and are providing real solutions for today and for the future, as the world grapples with the unprecedented burdens we have placed on our ecosystems and social systems. In the end either this new style will outperform the others — financially, socially, and environmentally — or it really won't matter, as humanity goes the way of the dinosaurs.

INVESTING ON THE
SUSTAINABILITY FRONTIER

BY PERRY ABBEY

In this chapter, Perry's investment approach is a little different. It's more a question of identifying the problems and then seeking out companies that will provide the solutions. Alternate energy and water purification are two areas that leap to mind. The investment metrics used to analyze these companies are a little different. He starts with the potential market, the capital resources available, and the ability of management to implement its vision.

W E'VE LOOKED AT THE IMPACT of large companies making small changes that have significant positive impacts for society. In a well-designed social impact investment portfolio, one would expect to have a healthy weighting in these kinds of companies. They will help provide some predictability of earnings and safety of capital that most investors require. But what about the really interesting emerging technologies and services that may provide the solutions that keep us alive as a species? Do we have to take on huge risk to invest in these companies? Well, the answer is yes — and no.

Modern Portfolio Theory (MPT), the darling of the investment industry for 50 years now, talks a lot about investing on the "efficient frontier." This is simply a process of trying to identify a portfolio that will most efficiently balance the volatility inherent in buying "risky" assets and the potential returns available from such investments over time. Of course modern portfolio theory is not adept at measuring the true risks and returns that such investments would entail using integrated or "triple bottom line" reporting. And we hope that the trend to reporting corporate performance on economic, social, and environmental parameters does continue and accelerate.

So perhaps its time to start looking at the risks and returns of investing on the "sustainability frontier." Here we will find the companies that are already profitably involved in near-term and interim solutions for our global woes, as well as the not yet profitable companies that may unlock immense benefits to this equation years and decades into the future. Conventional investment analysis will have an easy time with the "profitable" category, so let's look at a few examples of companies on the sustainable frontier.

Few rational folk these days doubt that global warming caused by our excessive use of fossil fuels is one of the most serious issues we must confront. And many of us believe that a transition to a benign hydrogen economy powered by clean fuel cells is the most attractive solution currently on the horizon. But these techno fixes may still be years and decades away and we need practical alternatives now.

Figure 4.1: Cumulative Installed Wind Power, Worldwide
Source: European Wind Energy Association[1]

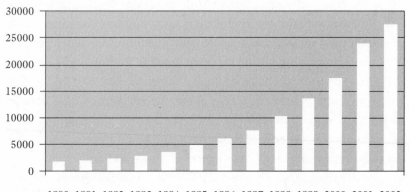

RENEWABLE ENERGY OPTIONS: WIND IN OUR SALES

Wind power is the fastest growing and cheapest renewable energy option. Advances over the last decade in turbine technology have brought the off-the-shelf cost of new wind installations down to a level that can compete directly with conventional fossil fuel generated power, dropping from levels of 35 to 40 cents per kilowatt hour in the 1980s to current levels of three to four cents per kilowatt hour. The economies of production scale will bring these price levels even lower in the near future, with the huge added benefit that the wind resource is quite predictable, inexhaustible, and, perhaps most critically, not in the control of any one company, country, or cartel. No one owns the wind.

The European Wind Energy Association recently launched an industrial blueprint, "Wind Force 12,"[2] with the objective of achieving 12 percent of the world's electrical needs from wind power by 2020. That's based on the assumption that global demand will also double by then. The study suggests that there are no technical, economic, or resource limitations to reaching this goal. And indeed, the goal of reaching an installed wind power base of 1,250 gigawatts by 2020 actually requires a smaller annual percentage increase than what we have seen over the last ten years. Technology improvements and recognition of some of the true costs of carbon-based power should make this goal even easier to attain.

As we move towards a hydrogen economy, wind is also likely to provide a key answer to the clean production of hydrogen. This notion of a clean energy loop or "Hydricity" (a term now trademarked by General Hydrogen Corporation), which uses clean renewables to produce hydrogen for fuel cell power generation when and where needed, is important to our ultimate replacement of fossil fuels.

Vestas: Doing the Right Thing

Enter Vestas Wind Systems. This Danish company (VWS on Copenhagen), is the world's largest manufacturer of wind turbines from a country with a long history of trying to do the right thing. Denmark has set itself very aggressive goals for supplying its power consumption needs from clean renewable sources. Recently Denmark passed a new milestone and now expects to supply 27 percent of its electrical needs from renewables (in 2003), with a target of 50 percent by the year 2030. A more comprehensive target for 2030 is to supply 35 percent of all energy requirements from renewables. That includes energy for heating, for automobiles, flying planes, industrial uses, and so on.

Figure 4.2: A Clean Energy Loop
Credit: Perry Abbey

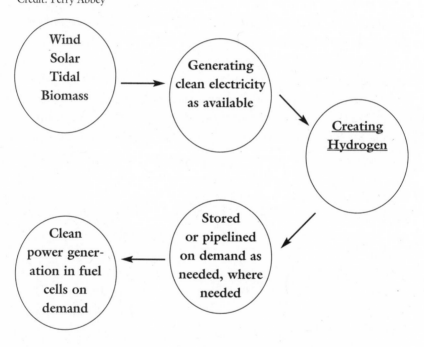

Vestas has had a healthy piece of this progress in Denmark and around the world with a current share of about 21 percent of the world's wind turbine market. Like most alternate energy and technology companies, Vestas' share valuations got way out of line during the technology market run up which ended in 2000. In today's more rational market place, it trades more like a value stock than the growth company it really is. Through the end of 2002, Vestas had a five-year average sales growth rate of 40 percent. 2002 was a difficult year, particularly in the US wind market which saw delays and more delays around government tax incentives for clean energy. As even the overtly oil-friendly administration in Washington recognizes the increasing need to cut dependence on foreign oil and is paying at least a little attention to renewables, I expect that more historic growth rates will resume for Vestas and the other major turbine producers. After three years of bear market mauling, consensus estimates from analysts covering Vestas have come way down, and as I write this, they are suggesting 15 to 16 percent earnings growth going forward at a time when the stock is trading at a multiple of 15 or 16 times next year's anticipated earnings.

CanHydro: A Triple-E Threat

Small is beautiful! While Vestas employs around 6,000 workers and has annual sales in the range of US$1.5 billion, other profitable companies on the Sustainability Frontier are quite small in comparison. Traveling from Copenhagen to Calgary lands us in the back yard of a tiny "green" utility company who are leading the way in Canada as consistently profitable producers of renewable source electricity. Canadian Hydro Developers (CanHydro, which trades as KHD on the Toronto Stock Exchange), generates power at 13 sites in Alberta, British Columbia, and Ontario. CanHydro uses predominately small scale "run of river" hydroelectric generation (59 percent of their production in 2002), or wind farms (40 percent). More wind and water projects are in development, as well as their first biomass plant in Northern Alberta.

John and Ross Keating, two brothers with a background in the oil patch but a vision of a sustainable future, founded CanHydro in 1989. John, with a finance background, raises the cash for a very capital-intensive business, and Ross, with an engineering background, gets to develop projects and spend the cash. Sounds like a perfect setup for some serious sibling rivalry! And to quote the brothers, they both love building these hydro and wind projects that keep generating power, and making money, 24 hours a day, even when they're sleeping!

Their business case is compelling. In their own words: "We both came from the oil and gas industry, with a junior oil and gas company where we got tired of riding the treadmill of depletion. Using a depleting resource like oil and gas, you have to keep using your cash flow to keep replacing the reserves and you still have to grow the company on top of that. It's very difficult and truly is a treadmill. But with renewable energy, if you add a hydro plant or a wind turbine, that's an energy source, just like an oil well, that doesn't deplete. And then the next year when you add another, you're reinvesting that cash flow in true growth."

On the alliteration front, CanHydro is a real "triple e"-rated company as they acknowledge the diversity of factors needed for a successful company (which naturally leads to successful shareholders). "You need to get the "e's" right," says Ross: economics, environment, and empowered employees. With this attitude, it's no wonder they won the 2001 award from Carleton University aimed at "rewarding creativity and innovation in making Canada a better place to live." Specifically, the award acknowledges that good management involves more than attention to the next quarter's financial report; it is also about preparing for the future through anticipating and reacting to economic, environmental, and social change.

So, an enlightened little utility with great vision and "ecologo-certified" power to sell. We look forward to seeing what direction they take as new technologies come on stream in the future. From the investors' viewpoint, CanHydro has 35 employees (I told you — small!), and net sales of about $16 million in 2002, and I'm talking preshrunk Canadian dollars here. Quite a different business model than Vestas.

Traditionally, investors in utilities are looking primarily for dividend returns rather than share appreciation. This is not the case with CanHydro, which does not pay a dividend. Since the average annual share price appreciation over five years has been 26 percent, this has not been a detriment to raising new equity capital. Of course, at some point in the next few years, the company's cash flow may become large enough to facilitate the kind of organic self-funded growth that investors really like to see. Green investors that like this corporate profile but are more interested in income than growth might look to the example of the Clean Power Income Fund, an environmentally friendly example of an "Income Trust" — an investment variety that has been sweeping the Canadian marketplace for the past few years in reaction to declining stock markets and declining bond yields.

Enviro-Friendly Energy Consumption: Clean Power Income Fund™

This income trust was launched in the fall of 2001 as a vehicle to provide unitholders with a dependable stream of tax-advantaged cash distributions from a set of environmentally-friendly power-generating businesses. It currently operates 40 different power generation facilities in both the US and Canada, producing about 14 percent from wind power, 11 percent from small scale hydro power, 27 percent from biomass, and 48 percent from biogas — the latter from US landfill sites, making something good from our overconsumptive ways! (See <www.cleanpowerincomefund.com>. The fund trades on the Toronto exchange under CLE.un.)

By the way, I've always been a bit confused by the concept of biomass power production — good or bad? — so I turned to Dermot Foley, a policy analyst in the Climate Change Program at the David Suzuki Foundation, for a simple explanation:

> "The use of biofuels can help reduce our dependence on fossil fuels and therefore help combat climate change. Unlike fossil fuels, which are buried deep in the ground, biomass is already part of the carbon cycle so it doesn't add any new greenhouse gases to the atmosphere. From a global perspective, if the sources of the biofuels are produced sustainably, this is good for the environment. On a local level, the use of biofuels can have a positive or negative impact on the immediate environment. For example, if a well-designed, cleaner-burning facility replaces a poorly operated and inefficient woodwaste burner, it can lead to an

improvement in air quality. A proper environmental assessment with meaningful public involvement is the best way to determine whether or not a biomass plant is appropriate for a local airshed."

Figure 4.3: Clean Power's Energy Map of North America: A better vision for the continent

Credit: Clean Power
And note how many spots on the game board are still available!

Clean Power's 40 renewable energy facilities:

◆ Biogas (GRS)   ■ Hydro

● Biomass   ▲ Wind

PROBYN ON POWER

Stephen Probyn is well known as an authority on renewable energy production so it was no accident that his company was chosen to manage the Clean Power Income Fund in 2001. In a phone interview in July 2003, Stephen said that he foresees great opportunities in this field driven by a confluence of factors, including:

- US concerns over Middle East oil impacting national security.
- State-level initiatives bringing in Renewable Portfolio Standards (RPS) mandating incremental targets for green energy production.
- Indigenous drivers coming from advances in renewable technologies and the underlying abundance of the resource itself, be it wind in Texas or geothermal and solar in Nevada.

He sees the real key to these drivers as the grassroots pressure from individual consumers who are demanding clean power and political action. The recently announced Ontario initiative for 3000 megawatts of new renewable supplies indicates that this pressure is building in Canada as well as the US. On his wish list would be production tax credits that would be easier to use and longer lived than they are currently, on the premise that companies need predictability before investing heavily in these new opportunities.

"AND NOT A DROP TO DRINK" — SUSTAINABLE WATER SOLUTIONS

I'm sure you've seen some of the chilling statistics on the looming water crisis on Planet Earth, which has been well documented in recent books such as *Blue Gold*[3] and *Water Wars*.[4] So how do we invest in sustainable water solutions? One opportunity is Zenon Environmental (ZEN on the Toronto exchange).

Zenon Environmental have positioned themselves to be the alchemists of the future, able to transform polluted, dirty water into liquid gold — clean water. By all accounts, access to clean, drinkable water is going to be one of the biggest challenges of the new millennium. Fresh water suitable for extraction makes up less than one percent of the planet's water. Given population and pollution pressures, this is a frightening thought — 1.3 billion human beings lack access to safe water; two billion have insufficient sanitation. Here's another frightening statistic: more people die every year from water-borne diseases than from wars.

Zenon will be one of the companies that governments and industries will be turning to in order to solve their water dilemmas. Zenon utilizes a unique membrane technology that can be used to turn polluted water into a potable drinking source. The technology can also be used to treat sewage and industrial effluents to create benign water that can be utilized for irrigation.

Zenon has focused on making its membrane technology into smaller, lower cost systems that are simple to use, thus making the technology globally accessible. The emphasis on small, easily-adaptable systems makes Zenon's membranes ideal for use in disaster-relief situations and humanitarian missions. Over 50 percent of the population in developing countries relies on polluted water sources. Zenon's membranes are currently used extensively by the Canadian Armed Forces on their peacekeeping missions.

Zenon's world headquarters in Oakville, Ontario showcases the possibilities that membrane technology can bring. All of the water that is used by the facility is treated on site and recycled back into the system for use in irrigation and flushing, reducing their water consumption by up to 85 percent. Here in Canada, the recent tragedies in Walkerton and North Battleford highlight the reality that even Canadians can't take access to safe water for granted. Zenon's products are leading the way to a safer, more sustainable world.

Zenon is in between Vestas and CanHydro with about 600 employees worldwide and 2002 revenues of 145 million of those pesky preshrunk bucks. The company has grown on average by 20 percent over the previous five years, just about mirroring the average increase in their share price over this period. Of interest to longer term value driven investors are their non-voting Class A shares (ZEN.a), which are less liquid and tend to trade at a discount of as much as 30 percent to their voting shares. The value proposition here is that this share class is scheduled to automatically convert to regular voting shares on June 10, 2008.

These three companies operating on the sustainability frontier are all examples of healthy profitable companies. While their share values will undoubtedly continue to fluctuate in the sometimes irrational equity markets, their profit history does tend to bring their investment risk profile down to a reasonable level. This is not a recommendation to trot out and buy these stocks tomorrow. Prudent asset allocation and diversification are always critical to investment success and for most investors professional management through a fund will be the intelligent route to the Sustainable Frontier — particularly when we start looking at the next group of companies!

These are the companies whose technologies have yet to meet with commercial success. These are the kind of "disruptive" technologies that can change the direction of history, and certainly cause huge problems for older technologies. The problem is, of course, that they are themselves susceptible to being leapfrogged in the race to success, hitting a dead end before their technology is accepted, or just plain running out of cash before they get anywhere close to profitability. And as anyone that still has a Betamax video player knows, the best technology is not necessarily the surviving technology. Let's look at two such companies in the alternate energy arena.

Alternative Energy: Interim Innovations

Westport Innovations is a small Vancouver-based company developing natural gas diesel engines designed primarily for the heavy transportation and power generation markets. Both of these potential market places are huge and in an era of ever tightening environmental standards, both are in need of cleaner technologies. While I don't believe that cleaner-burning natural gas is the ultimate energy solution we need, it is likely to be the most attractive interim approach over the next three or four decades — by which time, cleaner or zero impact technologies will, we hope, be the overwhelming reality. Westport has embarked on a joint venture with Cummins Inc. (the largest manufacturer of diesel engines for heavy use). Over the last few years, the joint venture company has sold some 3,000 spark-ignited natural gas engines for use in public transit and heavy trucks around the world. Impressive, but this is not the high pressure, direct injection technology that the company is really banking on.

A number of demonstration vehicles have been hauling trash for Norcal Waste Systems in the San Francisco Bay area for some time now in an application typical of the target market. Norcal currently has been testing 14 of the next generation engines with more on the way. They hope to convert their entire fleet of 38 heavy haulers to Westport's clean running technology, a move which will reduce their fleet emissions to the equivalent of taking 2200 cars off the road. That's real progress! California in particular has been at the leading edge of tightening air quality and emission standards and will surely figure prominently in Westport's ultimate business success or failure. And where California goes .... In a later chapter, Adine Mees will talk about Westport's vision from a different perspective — that of being a good corporate citizen as well as having a technology that may go a long way towards combating carbon emissions in a warming world.

Fuel Cells: Java or Jive?

The coffee shops around Vancouver have been a-buzz with talk about fuel cells for years now, ever since Ballard Power's share price started trending upwards in 1996 and 1997 and then went parabolic in early 2000. The tone of the conversations is a little more muted in summer 2003, as is the share price, but the underlying potential for their proprietary technology remains undiminished. Fuel cells, given a clean source for hydrogen, emit only power, heat, and clean water and have huge potential in overcoming global warming. Fuel cells are a scalable power source for everything from cars to generators or even laptop computers — and one whose only by-product is water vapor.

Of course, the issues here are around cost, technology adoption, and the source of the hydrogen to fuel them. The "clean loop" for hydrogen production I mentioned earlier would be the obvious choice but it may also take decades to achieve this reality. Reforming natural gas for hydrogen is likely to be an interim step, not as clean as we would like to see but an improvement over the infernal internal. Investors on the Sustainability Frontier will likely soon come to the conclusion that such a company is quite far up the slope — the potential return may be huge but that is tempered by such a high level of risk that Ballard may not be successful in bringing their fuel cells to market and achieving profitability. Like VHS and Betamax, there are several competing technologies and companies in the fuel cell race these days. Some of the other technologies may be better suited to larger scale industrial power installations or may be able to overcome their limitations around the automotive market that appears to be a likely area of success for Ballard. And the initial wave of hybrid gas/electric cars from Toyota and Honda may push commercial viability back for fuel cell cars.

Sustainable Goods: Interface Inc.

You're probably thinking by now that I'm totally focused on alternate energy and clean water. While I absolutely do think that these are two very critical areas for investors looking for a sustainable, just world, it is also simply a reaction to what I'm constantly asked for by new clients coming in my door the first time. We all understand the direct impact that dirty air and dirty water will have on the future if we don't invest in more sustainable approaches. But of course it goes far beyond these two avenues and we must look to companies that offer basic goods that may also be found on the sustainability frontier. One such company is a US manufacturer of commercial and institutional interiors. In other words, carpets, flooring, office furniture systems, and so on.

Interface Inc. (IFSIA on Nasdaq), has been in this business since 1973 when its founder, Ray Anderson, saw a niche for flexible or modular office floor coverings and began to produce carpet tiles for this market in 1974. In his words, "For the first twenty-one years of Interface's existence, I never gave one thought to what we took from or did to the Earth, except to be sure we obeyed all laws and regulations." Until 1994, at any rate, when he read Paul Hawken's book, *The Ecology of Commerce: A Declaration of Sustainability.* Ray realized that business as usual was simply not good enough and took it upon himself to fundamentally change the way Interface did business. He recognized then what seems obvious to us now — that "business is the largest, wealthiest, most pervasive institution on Earth, and responsible for most of the damage. It must take the lead in directing the Earth away from collapse, and toward sustainability and restoration."

Ray was also heavily influenced by the definition of a sustainable society as outlined in the book, *The Natural Step for Business*,[5] by Brian Natrass and Mary Altomare. Using this as a basis, Interface has specified their own seven-step approach to sustainability. This is a process to make change and has five technical steps, which are the easy ones to tackle, and two "systems" steps of which the last, "redesigning commerce" is a much longer recipe for change that goes far beyond the individual corporation.

1. **Eliminate waste**
   The first step to sustainability; QUEST is Interface's campaign to eliminate the concept of waste, not just to reduce it incrementally.
2. **Benign emissions**
   The focus is on the elimination of molecular waste emitted with negative or toxic impact into our natural systems.
3. **Renewable energy**
   The goal is to reduce the energy used by our processes while replacing nonrenewable sources with sustainable ones.
4. **Closing the loop**
   The aim is to redesign our processes and products to create cyclical material flows.
5. **Resource-efficient transportation**
   The objective is to find new methods to reduce the transportation of molecules (products and people), in favor of moving information. This includes plant location, logistics, information technology, video-conferencing, e-mail, and telecommuting.
6. **Sensitivity hookup**
   The vision is to create a community within and around Interface that understands the functioning of natural systems and our impact on them.
7. **Redesign commerce**
   The long-range target is to redefine commerce to focus on the delivery of service and value instead of the delivery of material. Interface Inc. is also engaging external organizations to create policies and market incentives that encourage sustainable practices.[6]

This is pretty heady stuff and Interface has had nearly a decade to implement this approach. It didn't happen overnight, since nobody in the company knew exactly what the new vision really meant. But in this case the most senior management of a large company had essentially empowered their employees to think outside the box and find a new paradigm for the company, using their conscience as a guide. So how have they done?

Aside from creating this eloquent template for change, the folks at Interface are not under any illusion that it is an easy task for a large multinational manufacturing "stuff" to meet these objectives overnight. They are making great progress, however. There is a vitality and enthusiasm in their workforce engendered by the inclusive nature of these steps. People want to come to work and there's a backlog of job applications. On the metrics side, Interface has reduced their carbon impact by 30 percent and has set an ambitious target of getting to 100 percent renewable energy sources by 2020. They also hope to be utilizing 50 percent reclaimed or renewable material inputs by 2007. I think they'll get there handily and then set their sights even higher. But perhaps their biggest contribution has been to lay out a process for all to see, one that can be implemented by any company on any continent.

BACK TO THE SUSTAINABLE FRONTIER: INVESTMENT ADVISORS

A somewhat different approach is taken by Innovest Strategic Value Advisors, an internationally recognized investment research and advisory firm specializing in analyzing nontraditional drivers of risk and shareholder value, including a company's performance on environmental, social, and strategic governance issues. Several independent commentators have recently recognized Innovest as the leading firm in the world in this area. Founded in 1998 with the mission of identifying nontraditional sources of risk and value potential for investors, the firm currently has over US$850 million under direct subadvisory mandates. Innovest also provides custom portfolio analysis and research to leading institutional investors including Schroders, State Street Global Advisors, Rockefeller & Co., as well as to pension funds such as CalPERS, British Petroleum, and ABP in the Netherlands.

Their view is that it is increasingly difficult to identify the true value of modern corporations as more and more of this value is hidden in knowledge-value and intangibles. Even into the mid 1980s, they suggest that financial statements tended to reflect at least 75 percent (on average) of the true market value of major corporations. Today's consensus would indicate that that number has dropped to 15 percent, which makes it incredibly difficult to make sound investment decisions. This has lead to Innovest's concept of the "Iceberg Balance Sheet," which is meant to focus on that 85 percent of corporate value which cannot be explained by traditional securities analysis. This approach is trying to measure intangible value drivers, including:

- "Eco-value"
- Human capital
- Stakeholder capital
- Sustainable governance

Hmmm ... wouldn't these be useful in getting closer to an integrated or "triple bottom line" for our corporate adventures on Earth! Well, Figure 4.4, is what they think this iceberg looks like.

While the depth and sophistication of Innovest's research capabilities put their data out of economic reach of individual advisors like me, they are rapidly gaining credibility with the large institutional investors as they assess these sustainability factors for specific companies and document financial outperformance. As social investing continues to gain market share, I look forward to seeing price efficiencies that will lead to having this kind of research capacity on every advisor's desktop, alongside broader social measures such as the MJRA and KLD databases, in much the same fashion that we take it almost for granted that we have access to a Bloomberg terminal or to Standard & Poor's or Valueline research to help us in making sound decisions. And when you really think about the veracity of such models as this "Iceberg Balance Sheet," you have to question whether or not the conventional investment industry research model is the one that is liable to leave you at risk

Figure 4.4: The Innovest Iceberg

Credit: Innovest Strategic Value Advisors

Financial Capital

Stakeholder Capital
- Regulators & Policymakers
- Local communities/NGO's
- Customer relationships
- Alliance partners

Human Capital
- Labour relations
- Recruitment retention strategies
- Employee motivation
- Innovation capacity
- Knowledge Development & Dissemination
- Health & Safety
- Progressive workplace practices

Strategic Governance
- Strategic scanning capability
- Agility/adaptation
- Performance indicators/monitoring
- Traditional governance concerns
- International "best practice"

Environment
- Brand equity
- Cost/risk reduction
- Market share growth
- Process efficiencies
- Customer loyalty
- Innovation effect

by overlooking some of the fundamental value-drivers in the capital markets today.

One final note: While I am not a statistics kind of a guy and won't be producing elaborate quantitative models of the Sustainable Frontier anytime soon, this is a burgeoning area of theoretical research. Innovest is not alone in showing hard evidence of financial outperformance by sustainability leaders. Others are busy coming to the same statistics-laden conclusions about the performance or out-performance of sustainability universes or indices. Not surprising really, and probably just a subset of the very numerous studies look-ing at the outperformance of SRI indices over the last decade or so. Given these studies and the sad state of the world of late, my only question is: Why would a prudent investor not want to apply social and sustainability parameters to their investments? Using them to leverage change in the world and change in your pocketbook. Global Profit and... well, I think you already noticed the book's title!

SHAREHOLDER POWER

UNLIKE THE COMPANIES REFERRED to in the previous chapters, many companies won't change unless we tell them to. Being a social investor is about using our voices and our influence as shareholders to make a positive difference in the companies we own. Over the years, social investors have discovered that shareholder activism is a far more powerful tool for social change than screening.

Because we are investors, it doesn't make sense to for us to embarrass or punish companies for poor social, environmental, or ethical performance. Instead, we must pressure them to address the social, environmental, and ethical issues that matter to us. To be effective, we must be aware of the challenges companies face in addressing these issues and offer concrete suggestions regarding ways they can overcome these obstacles to meet our concerns.

Sometimes dialogue is entirely consensual; other times it can get a little heated — but investors don't usually engage in conflict for conflict's sake. Our goal is to enhance shareholder value by helping the companies we own address these issues before they have a significant impact.

The tools shareholder activists use to have an impact on corporate performance are: direct dialogue with companies, filing shareholder resolutions, and proxy voting. Direct dialogue involves everything from asking simple questions to clarify your understanding of a company's social or environmental policies, to expressing concern over a specific issue, to conducting long-term, in-depth dialogues that involve multiple stakeholders.

Shareholder resolutions or proposals are a formal request for action that is voted upon at a company's annual general meeting (AGM). Resolutions are often cosponsored or co-filed with other social investors. The purpose of the resolution is to focus management attention on the issue and have them adopt policies or practices that will help reduce risk and increase shareholder and stakeholder value.

Proxy voting is one of the most important tools in this toolbox. Without support from many investors, important shareholder resolutions fizzle because they don't get enough votes. Every year, shareholders of publicly traded companies are called upon to vote on a series of resolutions concerning issues ranging from board membership and executive pay to social and environmental issues. As a shareholder (or mutual fund unitholder or pension beneficiary), you (or your mutual fund or pension fund), have a right to vote on these important issues.

The number of social resolutions being filed appears to be steadily increasing and, more heartening, is the increase in the level of support that they are receiving from shareholders. 2002 saw 802 shareholder proposals filed at the more than 2,000 US companies that the Investor Responsibility Research Center (IRRC) tracks regularly. Of these proposals, 273 were concerned with social issues and 147 of them came to a vote. Shareholder proposals, especially social issue proposals, traditionally get less than ten percent of the vote. 2001 saw 45 proposals garner double-digit support, while 2002 saw at least 23 proposals receiving over ten percent support, while 13 gathered over 20 percent support. This kind of support for social issue proposals hasn't been so widespread since the apartheid era, when proposals urging companies to stop doing business in South Africa were gathering widespread support.

Proposals that addressed concerns about global warming gathered an average of 18.8 percent, with companies such as American Standard, ExxonMobil, and General Electric witnessing over 20 percent support from shareholders for these resolutions. At least 45 proposals were filed in 2002 on global labor standards, while proposals on predatory lending and sexual discrimination were also popular. A number of proposals were dropped when management moved to address the issue before putting it to a vote. The year 2002 also saw a first for social issue proxies — a social issue proposal that was opposed by management won majority support.

The number of proposals for 2003 showed tremendous growth. At this writing, there had already been 1,034 proposals filed, at least 237 of which were on social issues. The environment (specifically global warming), and global labor standards were the two hot topics again, with 58 and 27 proposals filed respectively. Among electric utilities and oil and gas companies, the average support level for global warming proposals was 22.6 percent. According to the Investor Responsibility Research Center (IRRC), in the last 32 years the only proposals that received the same amount of support have been board diversity proposals in 2001 and 2002.

There has been a dramatic increase in the number of proposals that address corporate governance in response to the controversies surrounding Enron and WorldCom in 2002. Traditionally, proposals have been starkly divided between social issue proposals and corporate governance issues. But these trends have recently changed. According to IRRC's director of social issues, Meg Voorhes, "One notable trend is that the Enron disaster is accelerating a merger of interests between the worlds of corporate governance and social resolutions. This is a

departure from the past, when corporate governance and social resolution filers usually pursued very different agendas."

> It is clear that 2003 will be remembered as the year
> when investors decided to stand up and be counted,
> using their voice and vote to call for strengthened cor-
> porate governance and solid corporate citizenship.
> Investors are moving from passive holders of stock to
> becoming active and responsible owners ... under-
> standing the leverage they have as individuals and
> institutions who have invested their capital and faith in
> these companies.[1]
>
> — TIM SMITH, PRESIDENT OF THE SOCIAL
> INVESTMENT FORUM

The number of Canadian resolutions is far more modest than the
American statistics — a reflection of the relative size of the two markets and of the different levels of social activism. From 1982 to 1996
there were fewer than three proposals in each year. 2003 has seen 64
proposals so far, a number that is in line with the trend in shareholder activism over the last few years.[2]

There are a number of approaches to shareholder activism. Some
shareholders focus exclusively on engaging a company in dialogue.
This style has emerged from the UK where it is very difficult to file
shareholder resolutions. Shareholders have to elicit the support of
100 shareholders in order to file a resolution. In the absence of a
more activist option, UK shareholders have become very experienced
in the art of dialogue with corporations and achieved many successes. Canadian and US social investors usually incorporate filing shareholder resolutions with dialogue, often withdrawing a resolution in
exchange for an opportunity to engage in ongoing dialogue with the
company.

At Real Assets, our strategy has been aggressive. We think that
companies should be responsive to us as shareholders but we know
that most companies have to be hit over the head with something
before they respond so we usually start the process by filing a share-

holder resolution. That's a loud knock on the CEO's door and it seems to get a dialogue going with the company almost immediately. We file shareholder resolutions about issues that we think will help reduce risk and improve the performance of the companies in our portfolios. And we only withdraw if the company commits to making significant progress on the issue. As part of this growing trend, Real Assets filed resolutions in four issue areas last year. Responsible finance, international human rights, and two areas that we thought demanded attention immediately — climate change and responsible use of water.

Our approach to this is very issue oriented. That means that we identify a number of issue areas where we think that shareholder activism will reduce financial liabilities and add value, both financially and socially. We add to that list every year. As part of this, we do extensive research and collaborate with labor, NGOs, communities, and other stakeholders.

We start with issues related to broad international codes of conduct such as the International Labor Organization's Declaration on Fundamental Principles and Rights at Work, the CERES Principles, the McBride Principles, the Global Sullivan Principles, and the Organization of Economic Cooperation and Development (OECD) Guidelines for Multinational Enterprises — many of the same codes that CalPERs and NYCERs use to frame their concerns about long-term risk.

INTERNATIONAL CODES OF CORPORATE CONDUCT

The ILO Declaration of Fundamental Principles and Rights at Work upholds the notion that economic and social progress are irrevocably intertwined and confirms the role of the International Labor Organization in fighting for social justice while protecting workers' rights.

The CERES Principles are a set of principles that corporations can adopt to publicly affirm their commitment to being responsible, accountable stewards of the environment in every facet of their business, from waste management and energy conservation to employee safety and public reporting.

The McBride Principles are a set of principles designed to ensure proper representation and treatment of minorities — religious groups in particular — in order to eliminate discrimination in the hiring and management policies of companies in Northern Ireland.

The Global Sullivan Principles signify a company's commitment to operating in a socially responsible way that ensures protection of human rights for employees, communities and business partners while also signifying a dedication to sustainable development.

The OECD Guidelines for Multinational Enterprises are a set of voluntary guidelines that are intended to ensure the responsible actions of multinational corporations in regard to employee rights, environmental and community protection, and fair business practices.

INTERNATIONAL HUMAN RIGHTS

Real Assets filed our first shareholder resolution with Canadian oil and gas giant Enbridge. We were very concerned about potential human rights' risks arising from its operations in Colombia: Enbridge owns 25 percent of Ocensa, that country's most important pipeline. We were especially concerned that security providers for the company might be associated with Colombian paramilitaries.

The war in Colombia has killed more than 40,000 people in the past decade — mostly at the hands of paramilitaries — and it's the most dangerous place in the world for organized labor. We were able to withdraw the resolution when Enbridge agreed to adopt voluntary principles on security and human rights and to work with us on the implementation of those principles. Enbridge has also persuaded its Ocensa partners to adopt a new human rights policy and to adopt measures to promote human rights in Colombia, including renegotiating its agreement with the Colombian Ministry of Defense to reference human rights-related provisions.

Since Real Assets launched its campaign, Enbridge has directly intervened with the Colombian government in human rights-sensitive issues touching its operations, stepped up its efforts to educate employees and suppliers on the importance of human rights, and committed to developing credible monitoring and reporting systems. This will have a ripple effect through Colombia and through the Canadian oil and gas sector; ultimately, it will reduce liability for many of the other companies in our portfolio.

I mentioned the international coffee issue in Chapter One. We joined Oxfam and other NGOs and social investors to co-file a shareholder resolution calling on Procter & Gamble to do more to help the farmers who grow its coffee by purchasing a portion of its coffee beans from Fair Trade sources, signing up to international coffee quality standards and supporting a multilateral, multi-stakeholder initiative to address the structural causes of the current coffee crisis. As I mentioned earlier, the big four coffee roasters each generate more than US $1 billion in coffee sales — so if you're just worried about the next quarter, this probably isn't an issue given the profit margins. But it doesn't take a rocket scientist to recognize that deteriorating quality of product, environmental degradation in growing areas, potential brand risk because of human rights abuses — all of these things are issues for long-term shareholders in these companies. Besides, if Dunkin' Donuts can be part of the solution, the four biggest coffee roasters can, too!

CLIMATE CHANGE

A study of the international oil and gas industry by the World Resources Institute found that if they looked at the most-likely scenario for future environmental regulations, losses to shareholder value ranged from one percent to six percent of stock market capitalization among the companies studied. With the ratification of the Kyoto Protocol, investors must evaluate how companies are going to fare relative to their competitors in a carbon-constrained future. That's why we filed shareholder resolutions with the Canadian oil and gas companies, Nexen and Petro-Canada, calling for greater disclosure of the financial risks associated with greenhouse gas emissions, and for more details about how they're going to reduce those risks. We want to see that companies have concrete action plans in place that are both economically sound and good for the environment!

In recent years we've seen the US back away from the Kyoto Protocol. Interestingly enough, some of America's biggest businesses — companies such as DuPont and United Technologies — support action on climate change and want regulatory certainty on the carbon issue. These companies are not stellar corporate citizens but I think that their support for these issues is evidence of a change in corporate attitude. Companies with a long-term perspective can't afford to ignore these potential liabilities.

Nexen did agree to comply with our shareholder proposal once the rules of the game established by the Canadian government on Kyoto implementation are sufficiently clear. As a result of this, we withdrew the proposal. But even though Petro-Canada has an enviable record on environmental management systems, it was unwilling to provide assurance that it would comply with the shareholder proposal. Our proposal won 7.7 percent of the vote at the company's AGM held April 2003.

RESPONSIBLE FINANCE

Everyone loves to hate the banks and all of these issues come in to play when we talk about the banks. In many ways, the banks are among our most responsible corporate citizens: they give a lot back to the communities where they operate. But since the banks have debt or underwriting relationships with nearly every major company in North America, they've become a proxy for the social, environmental, and ethical risks inherent in the operations of those companies. And as they move more aggressively into the global arena, we need to be even more concerned about their risk management policies and practices.

The Carbon Disclosure Project Report was released in 2003 by a coalition of 35 institutional investors (including Merrill Lynch, Swiss Re, and the Credit Suisse group), who together manage over US$ 4.5 trillion. The report, produced by Innovest Strategic Value Advisors, found that climate change would have a major impact on financial performance, and could slash values by 40 percent for some heavy polluters. Banks would suffer a 29 percent decline in market value if they were to experience climate-change-related loan impairments of just ten percent — that means the bank stocks will tank if ten percent of their loans are doubtful collections. And that's not even considering the collateral damage to other companies that merely have to deal with the business consequences of erratic climatic conditions.

Once the banks start to take their social and environmental responsibilities seriously, they in turn will exert a powerful positive influence on their clients. For the past two years, we have been working with a coalition of responsible investors representing over $23 billion in socially screened assets to hold major global financial institutions — such as Citigroup and Morgan Stanley Dean Witter — accountable for the social and environmental impacts of their activities.

Citigroup has made steady progress in responding to the dialogue group's concerns, including the adoption of formal policies, public reporting, and training for its bankers on social and environmental risks. But the bank remains involved in some very controversial projects and hasn't provided detailed evidence that its bankers are living up to its own standards in concrete terms. The shareholder group has been in active discussion with the bank to provide constructive feedback on its annual sustainability reporting. At the end of 2002, a decision was taken by the shareholder group not to file in order to reward the company for forward progress, but to make clear that improvements, especially in the area of providing evidence that policies were actually working, would be needed to avoid a shareholder proposal for the 2004 AGM.

Since then, ten of the world's leading banks — including Citigroup, Barclays, ABN Amro, Royal Bank of Scotland, and Credit Suisse — have signed on to the "Equator Principles" to adhere to strict environmental and social impact standards when financing dams, power plants, pipelines, and similar infrastructure projects around the world. The principles came out of mounting pressure from protest groups as well as the ongoing dialogue with, among others, Friends of the Earth, Christian Brothers Investment Services, Trillium Asset Management, Ethical Funds, and Real Assets. Adherence to the principles is voluntary, and many don't think they go far enough but it's clearly a good first step in raising the bar for all the banks when they consider financing projects such as the Three Gorges Dam in China.

We learned a lot from our work with the coalition and in 2002–2003 we decided to bring the campaign home to Canada. About ten years ago, the big five Canadian banks signed on to an international agreement promising to incorporate social and environmental and ethical criteria into their lending and underwriting operations. They also promised to report on their progress periodically. Not one of them could send us a comprehensive report. So we filed shareholder resolutions with all five asking them to come clean about the criteria they use to assess companies vis-à-vis social and environmental and ethical liabilities.

Two of the Canadian banks were keen to move forward in this area so we withdrew our resolutions from The Bank of Nova Scotia and the Canadian Imperial Bank of Canada (CIBC). The Bank of Nova Scotia launched an internal review of its CSR practices and agreed to consider GRI reporting standards. CIBC agreed to board-level dialogue and to consider GRI reporting standards, and the Royal Bank said that it had moved this issue up on its agenda as a result of our shareholder resolution. We took our proposal to the vote at the Bank of Montreal's AGM and won 29.9 percent of the vote. This demonstrated extensive support by mainstream institutional investors. The company has agreed to return to the table to discuss social, environmental and ethical disclosure issues. We had a similar showing at the Toronto Dominion Bank AGM, winning 27.1 percent of the vote.

WATER

Water is one of the key sustainability challenges of the 21st century. You can't grow food or stay alive without water. If present consumption patterns continue, the UN predicts that two out of every three people on Earth will live in water-stressed conditions by the year 2025. This is an issue that is going to affect all of us.

Climate change and water are inextricably linked. As major rivers run dry, water tables are falling on every continent and the demand for water is exceeding the sustainable yield of aquifers around the world. Overpumping is now widespread in China, India and the US, which together produce half of the world's food. US companies can't afford to ignore this issue because the water is running out faster than they think. And Canadian companies can't afford to ignore it because guess who'll supply the water when the US runs out.

Businesses must assess the risks they face in an increasingly water-scarce world and address those risks through effective monitoring systems, active conservation efforts, the provision of equitable access to water resources, and better disclosure. The biggest risk is in ignoring this issue. Swiss Re, a major reinsurer, considers their clients' water management practices when assessing risk exposure.

From the corporate side, the companies that bottle water are complicit in a lot of the abuse, in spite of the fact that the success of their businesses is directly linked to their access to this precious resource. We were holding Coke and Pepsi in our portfolio so we cosponsored a shareholder proposal with Trillium Asset Management asking those companies to consider the new business risks posed by increasing freshwater scarcity around the globe, including the risk of community opposition to local bottling operations.

At a meeting held in January 2003 in Real Assets' Vancouver offices, Coca Cola provided evidence of good water management systems. It also promised that the company's 2003 environmental report will include information on its water-related performance, business risks arising from water scarcity, and efforts undertaken to mitigate water uses and impacts. Coke also passed on the results of an internal investigation into allegations of water overuse in Kerala, India. In response to this constructive approach to water issues, we were able to withdraw our shareholder proposal. We'll be monitoring Coke's progress with keen interest.

PepsiCo, on the other hand, responded poorly to our shareholder proposal in spite of the fact that 37 percent if its sales come from beverages. Not only was the company not forthcoming with information about its water use, it contested our proposal at the Securities and Exchange Commission (SEC). In February 2003 we won the Pepsi challenge when the SEC sided with Real Assets and

Trillium Asset Management and insisted that Pepsi include our resolution in its proxy materials. The resolution, the first of its kind,
received eight percent of the vote at Pepsi's AGM in May 2002 —
more than double the amount we needed to re-file again next year.

And speaking of Pepsi challenges, barely a week after the AGM
the New York Times reported that the village government of
Pudussery in southwestern India had revoked Pepsi's water-use
license. The license wasn't due to expire until 2005, but the community was concerned that Pepsi was overpumping local aquifers.
We just couldn't resist saying, "We told you so, Pepsi."

DOING WELL WHILE DOING GOOD: TRILLIUM ASSET MANAGEMENT

Trillium Asset Management was founded in 1982 to help demonstrate
that investing can promote social and economic justice while generating
solid returns. Now, two decades later, they can proudly tout a record of
accomplishment on both fronts. Socially screened portfolios have delivered competitive returns, and it has become widely accepted that
investors can do well while doing good. And they've gone beyond social
screening to focus on social change, through targeted community
investments that provide capital to the economically underserved and
through their shareholder advocacy initiatives.

When work was begun in the late '70s to form a whole company
dedicated to social and financial bottom lines, only isolated and scat-
tered efforts to avoid offending securities existed. The vision of the
founders of Trillium Asset Management was to catalyze a broader, more
comprehensive discipline within which investors could make decisions
based on probable social, environmental, *and* financial outcomes.

Whether working to protect forests or farm workers, Trillium has
found that the most powerful leverage for social change in the corporate
arena is the power of ownership in a company. Consider the results from
a small portion of its shareholder advocacy work in the past year alone:
In collaboration with environmental groups and other socially responsible investors, Trillium helped convince office products' giant Staples to
commit to stop selling products from endangered forests and to offer

more sustainable goods on their shelves — just as they did with The Home Depot a few years ago. In both cases, many of their competitors soon adopted similar policies. Chevron Texaco committed to develop a new global human rights program within a year after Trillium joined Amnesty International in filing a resolution asking the company to adopt a comprehensive human rights policy. And J.C. Penney joined the growing ranks of companies that Trillium has helped convince to prohibit workplace discrimination based on sexual orientation. In a rare move, J.C. Penney's board of directors asked shareholders to support our non-discrimination resolution, which won 93.3 percent of votes cast.

Trillium hasn't been alone in these efforts. Over the years, they've worked closely with other social investors (such as Real Assets), religious investors, pension funds, foundations, and non-profit organizations to define and strategize around issues. With like-minded pioneers, they cofounded the Social Investment Forum as a trade group for the socially responsible investment community. They also originated and incubated the Coalition for Environmentally Responsible Economies (CERES), a coalition of environmental groups, faith-based groups, and social investors. Some of the world's largest companies now follow the CERES Principles, which commit companies to improve environmental practices and publicly report their progress.

HAVE FAITH

In the '70s and '80s, South Africa was a major focal point for social investors. The churches were leaders in shareholder activism in the social investment movement. Religious investors in the US joined together in 1972 to become the Interfaith Center on Corporate Responsibility (ICCR). ICCR now represents 275 faith-based institutional investors with an estimated $110 billion in assets. Every year they sponsor over 100 shareholder resolutions on social and environmental issues.

In 1975, Canadian churches established the Taskforce on the Churches and Corporate Responsibility (TCCR) to address issues such as apartheid and human rights abuses in Chile and other countries. They were very successful in the '80s, when they used shareholder action to encourage Canadian banks to reject new loans to South Africa. In 2001, TCCR merged with nine other interchurch coalitions to form KAIROS, an ecumenical organization dedicated to promoting human rights, justice, and peace.

The Churches Challenge Talisman on Sudan Operations

The risk to companies that ignore the potent force of shareholder action is evidenced by the tale of Calgary energy company Talisman and its involvement in the Sudan. In 1998 the company acquired a 25 percent share in an oil development located in the Sudan, the site of a terrible civil war that had resulted in the deaths of two million civilians. TCCR represented Canadian churches, church pension funds, and religious orders that owned shares in Talisman.

Representatives of the Taskforce on the Churches and Corporate Responsibility first approached the company shortly after it announced its intention to invest in the Sudan, to express concern about the company's plan to operate in a conflict zone in partnership with a regime accused of gross and systematic human rights abuses. Talisman was largely unresponsive, and church investors filed a shareholder proposal asking the company to produce independently-verified proof that its actions in the Sudan did not contribute to human rights abuses and the civil war. Talisman Energy refused to circulate the proposal, but church shareholders continued to press the company, which was by now under mounting pressure from a broad array of international agencies connected to relief operations in southern Sudan, where the humanitarian situation continued to deteriorate.

Shareholder efforts to engage Talisman gained significant momentum with the addition of institutional heavyweights — the New York City Employees Retirement System (NYCERS) and the New York State Common Retirement Fund. The shareholder proposal was re-filed the following year and received unprecedented support at the annual general meeting, garnering 27 percent of the vote, a record for a Canadian social issues proposal at the time.

Investor unease about Talisman's involvement in the Sudan led to a relentless divestment of Talisman stock. The California Public

Employees' Retirement System (CalPERS) sold its more than 200,000 shares in Talisman; the State of New Jersey divested its 680,000 shares; TIAA-CREF, a college teachers' fund, sold its 261,000 shares; and the Texas Teachers Retirement Fund divested its 100,000 shares. Investment analysts estimated that Talisman's share price dropped at least 15 percent in direct response to the divestment campaign.

Under constant pressure from shareholders and human rights groups, as well as a move in the US Congress seeking to de-list companies that did business in the Sudan, Talisman eventually sold its Sudanese assets in March of 2003. The company admitted that shareholder pressure and the alarming drop in share value caused by the publicity surrounding the Sudan had convinced them to sell off their assets.

The Churches Challenge Imperial Oil on Climate Change Risks

Carrying on the historic work of the Task Force on the Churches and Corporate Responsibility, the KAIROS coalition facilitated the joint efforts of the Presbyterian Church in Canada, Fonds Elisabeth-Bergeron (Soeurs de St. Joseph de Saint-Hyacinthe), and the Congregation of the Sisters of Saint Anne in filing a shareholder proposal with Imperial Oil. For the churches, the pressing issue of climate change has profound ethical implications, which is a matter of international and intergenerational justice.

Nancy Palardy is the program coordinator of corporate issues for KAIROS: Canadian Ecumenical Justice Initiatives, which is revitalizing the work and commitment of the churches and religious orders in Canada. Speaking to me in 2003, she explained their position thus: "While the change in our global climate is due in large part to the polluting emissions of rich industrialized countries, the consequences will be suffered disproportionately by poorer developing nations and by future generations. In addition to this justice perspective, the churches, as institutional investors, are also concerned about the potential impact that climate change will have on social development, economic growth, corporate cost structures, and stock market valuations. For integrated oil and gas companies such as Imperial Oil, these developments pose significant potential financial liabilities."

It is in light of these considerations that the three religious institutions requested that Imperial Oil prepare a report to share-holders detailing the range of potential financial liability associated with its greenhouse gas emissions. As the first proposal filed in Canada on climate change risk, the filers were pleased with the results of the vote. Although ExxonMobil holds 69.6 percent of Imperial Oil's shares (and voted against the proposal), of the remaining individual and institutional investors, 28.67 percent voted in support of the resolution. Given this level of support, the churches will continue their dialogue with the company and engage in discussions with other institutional investors that are identifying this as a key issue of fiduciary and corporate social responsibility.

RECORD VOTE ON SWEATSHOP LABOR ISSUE

At Real Assets, we frequently collaborate with other shareholder activists such as the Shareholder Association for Research and Education (SHARE) and Ethical Funds. SHARE coordinates the efforts of pension funds in Canada and has been a leader in Canada on the issue of sweatshop labor. We co-filed with several institution-al investors on an anti-sweatshop resolution with the Hudson's Bay Company (HBC). It won unprecedented support at HBC's AGM in May 2002, receiving almost 37 percent of the vote, which was at that time the largest vote in Canadian history in favor of a share-holder proposal dealing with a social or environmental issue. The message to HBC was clear: public concern over sweatshops isn't going to go away and investors are demanding that they deal with this issue. Since then HBC has committed to building internal capacity to address the labor standards of its overseas suppliers, out-lined a credible approach to public reporting, and is revising sections of its vendor code to bring it closer to the International Labor Organization's conventions. We're not sure if this will prove to be adequate, but we do know that HBC must pay attention or risk potential consumer boycotts, litigation, or damage to its reputation and ultimately its brand.

RECORD ENVIRONMENTAL VOTE ON GREENHOUSE GAS EMISSIONS

Ethical Funds Inc. (EFI) is Canada's largest socially responsible mutual fund company. One of Canada's pioneers in social investing, Bob Walker is responsible for SRI policy and research at EFI and directs the company's shareholder activities.

In 2003, Ethical Funds Inc. filed a resolution with the steel manufacturing corporation IPSCO, asking the company to make use of existing guidelines on the reporting of toxic and greenhouse gases — guidelines sponsored by the federal government of Canada. IPSCO is the only large industrial emitter of toxic and hazardous substances that does not allow Environment Canada to publicly disclose the company-specific emissions from its facilities. This is in contrast to the company's practice of voluntarily disclosing emissions data from its US facilities under the Toxic Release Inventory (TRI) operated by the Environmental Protection Agency in the US.

At IPSCO's AGM in April 2003, the Ethical Funds Inc. resolution garnered 49.2 percent of the vote, beating SHARE's record vote at the Hudson's Bay Company and setting a new record in North America for an environmental proposal. Upon announcing the results of the vote, IPSCO stated that the board of directors would give full consideration to adoption of the proposal at its next meeting.

> What gets measured gets managed. What gets disclosed gets reduced. Reducing emissions reduces potential risks and liabilities. Ethical funds believes that the adoption of a policy of disclosing emissions data would be in the best interest of IPSCO employees, the best interests of the communities where IPSCO locates its plants, and in the best interests of future generations. We're gratified that nearly a majority of IPSCO shareholders agree.
> — BOB WALKER, VICE-PRESIDENT SRI POLICY
> AND RESEARCH, ETHICAL FUNDS INC.

NONGOVERNMENTAL ORGANIZATIONS (NGOS)

SWM seeking jaded institutional shareholders for a bold new journey into the murky world of applied ethics.

That's how Gavin Edwards suggested that he be introduced. But to give the lad a shred of credibility, I should probably mention that he's a forest campaigner with Greenpeace Canada — which means that he works on Canadian and international forestry issues, focusing mainly on markets and investment campaigns. With the growing success of shareholder campaigns, it's no surprise that NGOs are pressuring the investment community to live up to their responsibilities as shareholders. NGOs are recognizing that we need multiple strategies and they are playing a pivotal role in shareholder activism. Friends of the Earth is a key player in promoting dialogue on responsible banking initiatives; Oxfam initiated the coffee campaign; and Greenpeace has always been among the more creative forces in the NGO community.

In May 2000, Greenpeace Canada initiated a campaign to target mutual fund companies with holdings in two British Columbia-based logging companies (Interfor and West Fraser Timber). Both companies had withdrawn from a conflict resolution process aimed at striking a peace agreement with environmental organizations around logging of the Great Bear Rainforest, and instead continued logging in key pristine rainforest valleys in the region.

The campaign focused on dialogue with the mutual fund companies that had invested in these logging companies. According to Gavin, "Divestment of shares was always seen as a last resort. Our primary goal was to promote a dialogue between investors and logging companies in order to influence their logging decisions. But dialogue can only go so far, and when faced with an intransigent logging company and the possibility of mounting controversy in the highly competitive mutual fund marketplace, some companies decided to divest."

Ethical Funds Inc. decided to sell its $1.5-million holding. "At the time we viewed West Fraser as an eligible investment precisely because it was involved in a major effort to preserve temperate rainforest and end the war in the woods," said Bob Walker, vice-president of SRI policy and research at Ethical Funds. "But when the company withdrew from the dialogue process, we had little choice but to divest."

In early December, Friends Ivory Simes (FIS) of the UK followed suit, divesting over seven million dollars in Interfor shares following a Greenpeace briefing. Karina Litvack, director of research for FIS stated that: "Our clients have expressed their concern for conserving the world's forests and recognize the importance that these have in protecting our global ecosystem and combating climate change. We particularly commend companies that demonstrate a commitment to sustainable forestry, whether through their wood purchasing policies or forest management practices. Conversely, we view with concern companies which appear to overlook the risks that poor forestry practices, or poor wood procurement policies, can pose to their own long-term profitability."

Following the placement of ads in Vancouver and Toronto which profiled mutual fund company investments in the two logging companies, the Royal Bank of Canada decided to divest its Interfor holdings (excluding indexed funds) amounting to about $4 million. Friends Ivory Simes' and the Royal Bank's divestments represented almost ten percent of Interfor's outstanding shares — a significant share movement as a result of the campaign.

Not all institutional investors responded positively. For example, Toronto Dominion Bank (TD), which invests in both companies as well as providing credit for Interfor, clarified their position on the issue by stating that their investment decisions "may preclude the rejection of investments on moral or ethical grounds." A subsequent campaign was launched by Greenpeace during the mutual fund buying season in 2001, aimed at influencing mutual fund investors of TD Bank and other mutual fund companies in order that they could make a more informed investment decision. A huge banner was hung from TD's Toronto headquarters with images of the Great Bear Rainforest projected onto it to catch the attention of evening commuters in downtown Toronto — many of whom would be considering which mutual funds to purchase at that key time of year. Prime time media coverage of the event reached a far wider audience.

Finally, in April 2001, after considerable pressure from customers and investors (including buyers in Europe, North America, and Japan), Interfor and West Fraser agreed to a package of deferrals on logging, protection of rainforest areas, and an ongoing process to reform logging practices along with other BC logging companies. This came after months of discussions with Greenpeace and other environmental organizations. On the eve of its election call, the BC government endorsed the agreement, and though the government was subsequently voted out, the current government continues to endorse and implement the peace agreement (despite its general anti-environmental agenda), in large part because they understand the economic dynamics that delivered the peace agreement.

GLOBAL SHAREHOLDER ACTIVISM: SOUTH AFRICA

Since we're talking about global investing and social investing has its modern roots in investor and consumer campaigns in South Africa in the '70s and '80s, it seems fitting to end this chapter with a look at what's happening there more than two decades later.

Unfortunately, despite its long history of broad-based political activism, South Africa hasn't seen the emergence of a significant local shareholder activism movement. But there are a few important activism initiatives, and momentum is gradually building up among mainstream fund managers.

In spite of having its share of corporate governance disasters, shareholder activism is at a very early stage. Most assets managers don't have proxy voting policies, don't vote on all issues at AGMs (let alone attend them), and don't try to influence companies' social, environmental, and ethical performance.

There are a number of reasons for this apathy. First, asset managers are not convinced that the benefits of comprehensive shareholder activism outweigh the costs involved. Second, they don't recognize their power to influence corporate behavior and the responsibilities that come with this. And finally, there are other impediments — such as negative past experiences with various types of social investments (other than activism), the lack of a clear regulatory framework, a lack of institutional or retail demand, and the absence of a robust activism infrastructure (such as the type of social research conducted by MJRA and KLD or proxy voting services such as those provided by Institutional Shareholder Services (ISS).

The Community Growth Fund (CGF), South Africa's first activism fund, was launched in 1992 by a group of trade unions and currently has over R900 million under management. Every potential portfolio company is screened according to eight criteria: job creation, workforce training, corporate citizenship, environmental practices, safety standards, employment equity, corporate social responsibility, and labor relations. There are currently over 100 qualified companies in the CGF universe — not bad since it started out with 20. The CGF has also begun to encourage union representatives to vote their proxies and attend AGMs.

The other major social investing initiative in South Africa is the Earth Equity Fund, launched in 2001 by Frater Asset Management. An overlay of engagement (by proxy voting, direct meetings with management, and shareholder resolutions) is applied to the unrestricted investment universe. A detailed proxy voting policy has been developed and the fund votes at all AGMs, and publishes its voting record on its website. Frater starts the process by researching the company's corporate citizenship practices, and subsequently sets priorities for engagement based on input from an independent advisory board. The engagement strategies are based on position papers that have been completed in three priority areas — corporate governance, black economic empowerment, and HIV/AIDS. Filing a shareholder resolution is considered a last resort. So, in spite of strong activist roots, it's early days for shareholder activism in South Africa. But it is evolving as it has in the UK and North America.

The King Report on Corporate Governance in South Africa, released in March 2002, recommends that institutional shareholders — who have "been noted for their apathy towards participating actively in shareowner meetings" — set proxy voting policies, attend and vote at meetings, and make their policies and voting records publicly available.

There's more good news! The pioneering activities of dedicated shareholder activists such as Frater Asset Management are being increasingly recognized by government, the media, corporations, and clients.

HELP FOR THE INDIVIDUAL INVESTOR

It's clear that shareholders can have a tremendous impact on the social, environmental, and ethical performance of companies. But how does the average person make use of this effective tool for change? It's difficult, if not impossible, for individual investors to do adequate research in order to responsibly vote their proxies or to file shareholder resolutions on issues that are important to them. Fortunately, there are a number of fund companies in Canada and the US that do this important work. As an investor, you can be part of the solution by owning those mutual funds. For further information on how you can make a difference, see the Resources section at the back of this book.

MOSQUITOS FOR CHANGE: CONSUMER ACTION

If you think you're too small to have an impact, try going to bed with a mosquito in the room.
— Anita Roddick, founder of The Body Shop

THE GROWING TREND IN THE western world is to ask corporations to deal with issues that governments refuse to tackle — issues such as child labor and slavery, environmental degradation, Fair Trade, and so on. With governments becoming increasingly reluctant to put restrictions on business, consumer activism is one of the ways that citizens can affect global and national social policy. In some ways, it's becoming better to shop than to vote.

> Pressure groups are besieging American companies, politicizing business and often presenting executives with impossible choices. Consumer boycotts are becoming an epidemic for one simple reason: they work.
> — "BOYCOTTING CORPORATE AMERICA"
> *THE ECONOMIST*[1]

Consumer boycotts are a social dilemma that pits the needs of the individual against the needs of society. Consumers are faced with the choice of not buying a product that they want or need in order to improve the well-being of society or the environment or both. A person's feeling of community with the outside world challenges the selfish desires of individuals — so the decision to participate in a boycott is in many ways the victory of altruism over selfishness.

> Boycotts have become a pervasive and potent instrument of consumer discontent in today's marketplace. Consumers are increasingly willing to withhold patronage to curb perceived market abuses and/or increase corporate sensitivity to their economic, political, and social concerns.
> — SANKAR SEN, ZEYNEP GURHAN-CANLI, AND VICKI MORWITZ, *JOURNAL OF CONSUMER RESEARCH*[2]

The first boycott was in the 1880s. The Irish Land League organized a campaign for reform of the system of landholdings. They demanded that Captain Charles Cunningham Boycott give them a substantial reduction in their rents. He refused and as a result, the President of the Land League, Charles Stuart Parnell, called on the local people to stop having dealings with him. Laborers would not work for him, local shops stopped serving him (food had to be brought in from elsewhere for him and his family), and he even had great trouble getting his letters delivered. In the end, his crops were harvested that autumn through the help of fifty volunteers from the north of the country, who worked under the protection of nine hundred soldiers. The events aroused so much passion that his name became an instant byword. It was first used — in our modern sense of collective and organized ostracism — in the *Times* of London in November 1880 and within weeks it was everywhere.[3]

Since then we've broadened the concept of boycotts to include expressions of solidarity, where the costs are experienced by the consumer but the benefits belong to someone else. Think of the boycott of South African goods that preceded widespread international sanctions in the 1990s. Companies threatened by boycotts are generally motivated by the financial consequences of damage to reputation.

The Internet has dramatically changed the face of consumer boycotts, making the quick dissemination of information and strategies possible. "Getting the message out" has been made infinitely easier with the power of websites and e-mail and as a result consumer boycotts are becoming increasingly popular. The web is full of information on boycotts, from how to be a virtual activist (<www.netaction.org/training/>, <www.progressiveportal.org>) to websites entirely dedicated to listing current boycotts (<www.boycottcity.org>, <www.boycotts.org>). There are numerous sites, chatrooms, and message boards where consumers can trade beefs about products and companies that are unethical, inefficient, misleading, or just plain bad.

The future of boycotts will get even more tech savvy, as future generations of consumers are being raised on the Internet. The National Center for Education Statistics in the US states that the percentage of elementary and secondary schools that had Internet access in 1996 was 61 percent and 77 percent respectively. By 2000, these numbers had jumped to 97 percent and 100 percent.

BOYCOTTING BURMESE GOODS

There are currently hundreds of boycotts going on, with targets ranging from companies to entire countries. Of the current boycotts, perhaps the most successful has been the boycott in support of democracy in Burma (Myanmar).

PepsiCo came under extreme pressure from consumer groups for its involvement with the ruling military junta of Burma during the '90s. Pepsi's factories in Burma were being run by forced laborers in appalling conditions. To make it even worse, the factory owner had close ties to the military junta and actively fought against democracy.

Free Burma, a coalition of people dedicated to returning Burma to the democratic state that had been crushed by the military junta, was the genesis behind the Pepsi boycott. Free Burma engaged consumers by publicizing the controversy around Pepsi's continued presence in Burma. The boycott utilized the rapidly growing power of the

Internet to spread the word. Student organizations became involved and, as students are a target market for Pepsi, they were able to exert great pressure on the company. More than a hundred universities participated in the boycott, with well-known universities such as Harvard and Stanford declining million dollar deals with Pepsi because of its Burmese operations. Eventually the company was forced to cut all ties with Burma in order to avoid a public relations nightmare and on January 15, 1997, PepsiCo pulled all of its operations out of Burma.

PepsiCo was just one of many companies that Free Burma targeted for doing business with the military regime. Free Burma also used boycotts — or the threat of boycotts — to convince a number of other multinational companies to bail out of Burma. Among the companies that were forced to abandon their operations in Burma were Motorola, Apple Computers, Hewlett-Packard, Walt Disney, J. Crew, and Heineken.

These boycotts are beginning to bite economically. US apparel imports from Burma dropped 27 percent between 2001 and 2002, according to US Department of Commerce figures. Burma's 1991 Nobel Peace Prize recipient Aung San Suu Ky has called for companies to avoid the country, saying that sanctions "send a strong economic and political message" to the military regime.

Levi-Strauss Inc.

"It is not possible to do business in Burma without directly supporting the military government and its pervasive violations of human rights." (Levi-Strauss & Co., upon withdrawing from Burma.)

Adidas

"Adidas-Salomon is very concerned about the human rights record of the military regime in Burma/Myanmar. Consequently we stopped sourcing products from there in 1999.... None of our products have been made there since."

BHS (British Home Stores)

"Having reviewed the BHS supply chain, I can confirm that there were historical ties with a supplier in Burma. This link is now terminated and there will be no further business conducted within Burma."

IKEA

The IKEA group decided in May 1999 not to conduct business in Burma, stating that it is IKEA's position "to destroy any products from Burma at our warehouse locations."

Heineken and Carlsberg

Heineken cited public opinion and media attention as the reason why they withdrew a $30 million investment in Burma. Carlsberg cited the same reasons for canceling plans for a new factory in Burma.

BAILING OUT OF BURMA

Companies that have either left Burma, or publicly stated that would not invest in or source from Burma, include:

adidas-Salomon	Fenwick	Liz Claiborne
Anheuser-Busch International (Budweiser)	Fila	London Fog
	Foster's	Motorola
	Grattan	New Look
Ann Summers	H&M	Northwest Airline
Apple Computer	Heineken	Oracle
Arcadia Group	Hewlett-Packard	Oshkosh B'Gosh Inc.
Bank of Nova Scotia	Himalayan Kingdoms Ltd.	PepsiCo
British Home Stores		Phillips Electronics
The Burton Group	IBM	Polo Ralph Lauren Company
Carlsberg	IKEA	
Clarks	Interbrew (Labatt's)	Reebok
Compaq	Jansport	Royal Dutch Shell
Disney	John Lewis	Sara Lee
Ericsson Explore Worldwide, Ltd.	J Sainsbury	Seagram
	Kookai	
Federated Stores (Bloomingdales, Macy's)	Kuoni	
	Levi-Strauss & Co.	

TEXACO TUMBLES TO BLACK BOYCOTT

The boycott of Texaco in 1996 was another successful display of consumer power. A suit alleging discrimination by management against black employees had been filed two years earlier. The boycott was instigated by the discovery of tape recordings of Texaco executives belittling black employees. The reaction from the black community in the US was immediate. A massive boycott of Texaco had an immediate impact on the profits and the public image of Texaco. Just 11 days after the boycott began, the company capitulated and settled the lawsuit. Texaco agreed to pay $115 million to around 1,400 current and former employees and also pledged to give black employees a ten percent raise. The company also pledged to spend $35 million on a task force to investigate how to open up more opportunities for black employees, monitor racial discrimination, and provide diversity and sensitivity training.

FOREST STEWARDSHIP COUNCIL AND THE MARKETS INITIATIVE

The fact is, consumers find it hard to work together and collaborate even though individuals working together have tremendous clout. Organizing can be difficult, especially where the socially or environmentally destructive practices are obvious but consumers have little direct influence. Sectors such as forestry, mining, and energy have little direct contact with the general public.

That's what makes market campaigns such as those focused on protecting old growth forests so exciting. By the early 1990s, increasing concern over long-term destruction of old growth forests, both in the tropics and in temperate zones such as the forests of British Columbia led to increasingly bitter standoffs between environmentalists and logging companies. The problems were getting worse, but thankfully there were solutions in sight. In 1993 the Forest Stewardship Council developed standards for responsible management of timber resources. The trick was to educate individual consumers to spark demand for responsibly managed wood products. By 1997, studies showed that 35 percent of respondents rated environmental impacts as being either "very" or "extremely" important when buying a wood product — 67.3 percent said they would be willing to pay five percent more for certified wood products; 28.3 percent reported they would pay ten percent more; and 13 percent said they would pay more than ten percent.[4]

But consumer willingness wasn't translating into appropriate incentives for producers, because individual consumers didn't set the agenda for the industry. Instead, bulk purchasers of wood products acted as gatekeepers for consumer demand, providing what they thought the market wanted. Without the option of expressing a choice for environmentally friendly products, the free market wasn't delivering the right signals.

To resolve this problem, a coalition of environmental groups and shareholder activists decided to complement their direct action against timber companies by encouraging retailers and other bulk purchasers of wood products to avoid buying timber, pulp, or paper products sourced from environmentally sensitive areas.

By December 1998, 27 US corporations — including IBM, Dell, Kinko's, Nike, Levi-Strauss, Mitsubishi Motors America, Mitsubishi Electric America, and others — announced their commitments to stop selling or using old growth wood. Europe's largest home improvement center, B&Q, removed nearly all the old growth wood from its shelves. A major victory came in 1999 with Home Depot's announcement that they would end the sale of endangered wood by 2002 and seek to sell products certified as produced by sustainable methods. Commitments from other big wood retailers such as Lowes came fast on their heels. IKEA encourages all its suppliers to source their wood from operations with certification from the Forest Stewardship Council. Wood accounts for 75 percent of the material used in IKEA products, which means that the company's commitment to ensure that all its wood products come from verified well-managed forests is all the more significant.

When Michael Jantzi and I co-authored a book in 2001, we asked our publisher to print it on recycled paper. The publisher hadn't had a request for recycled paper in more than two years. We were shocked. We assumed that most publishers used recycled paper. When the book sold out early, we weren't able to reprint because the printer didn't keep recycled stock on hand. Nicole Rycroft of the Markets Initiative has taken care of that little problem. (The Markets Initiative is a coalition project of the Friends of Clayoquot Sound, Greenpeace Canada, and the BC Chapter of the Sierra Club of Canada.) Nicole has worked extensively with Canadian book publishers to help them shift away from papers derived from the world's ancient and endangered forests.

As large consumers of paper, publishers have significant potential to safeguard biodiversity and the world's forests. Seventy-one percent of the world's paper supply is derived from ecologically valuable, biologically diverse forests — 40 percent of BC's ancient temperate rainforests (including global treasures such as the Great Bear Rainforest and Clayoquot Sound) and 65 percent of Canada's boreal forests are logged to produce paper. With global paper consumption projected to increase roughly 50 percent by 2010, shifting major paper consumers to more environmentally responsible purchasing practices is integral to turning the tide against forest destruction. Markets Initiative has worked throughout the entire publishing supply chain for the past two and a half years — with publishers, writers, printers, and mills — to find and develop ancient forest-friendly papers.

In 2000, no Canadian book publishers were consistently printing on recycled papers. There were no printers stocking ancient forest friendly papers and an ancient forest friendly book grade paper was not regularly available. The first large order of these papers was placed and financially underwritten by New Society Publishers, the publisher of this book. They paved the way for other North American publishers to start printing their books on ancient forest friendly papers.

As of 2003, 35 leading Canadian publishing houses have formalized commitments to eliminate their use of papers originating from the world's ancient and endangered forests. These publishers include McClelland & Stewart, Random House Canada, Penguin Canada,

Raincoast Books, Douglas & McIntyre, Key Porter Books, and New Society Publishers.

The conundrum of the lack of availability of suitable papers because there was no market for them and the lack of publishers ordering ancient-forest-friendly papers because none were available was resolved by having publishers make formal policy commitments to shift their purchasing over a period of time. Publishers alerted their paper suppliers that they would do business with those who fulfilled their new paper needs and a market was born. Seven ancient-forest-friendly papers have since been developed for Canadian publishers and are now available internationally. Five Canadian book printers now stock a variety of these eco-friendly papers.

HARRY POTTER CASTS A SPELL
ON THE PAPER INDUSTRY

Exemplifying the effect of these ancient-forest-friendly policies is the publication of *Harry Potter and the Order of the Phoenix* on ancient-forest-friendly paper. The Canadian edition, published by Raincoast Books, is the only one internationally to be printed on paper free of endangered-forest fiber.

By printing the initial run of 935,000 copies of *Harry Potter and the Order of the Phoenix* on 100 percent post-consumer recycled, processed chlorine-free paper, Raincoast Books have saved:

- 29, 640 trees
- 47,007,044 liters of water (12,221,831 US gallons — enough to fill 31 Olympic-sized swimming pools)
- 633,557 kilograms of solid waste (1,406,497 pounds — equivalent to 155 average female elephants)
- Electricity to power the average home for 195 years
- Greenhouse gases equivalent to driving a car 3.9 million kilometers (2,423,460 miles)

Markets Initiative's work with Canadian book publishers has created a cross industry shift and sparked an international movement with book publishers in six other countries. Publishers' actions are inspiring awareness in readers, booksellers, printers, and writers of the value of the world's ancient forests and the potential that we all possess to create positive change.

The results of the Markets Initiative have been dramatic — and are likely to continue for the foreseeable future. According to a recent study of major purchasers of British Columbian forest products conducted by IBM business consulting services, there is clear evidence of a "greenward shift in procurement policies." Not only are larger producers beginning to clean up their act as a result of buyer pressure, but smaller producers of environmentally-sustainable wood products are gaining access to markets that would have been closed to them before. Producers have to pay attention because the buyers believe that the greenward shift is real and will continue into the future. But the sustainability of the shift relies on continued customer pressure for greener products.[5]

ECO-CERTIFICATION

Forest Stewardship Council certification provided the benchmark that the Markets Initiative needed to bring companies on side. Certification is a market-based initiative that assists consumers to make informed choices and gives businesses that sell certified products a clearly defined market advantage. Eco-labels are an important part of the certification process. The www.eco-labels.org website suggests that good eco-labels should have clear and concise standards, independent verification, and a certification body that is independent of the industry. One of the best known examples of an eco-label is Earthtrust's Flipper Seal of Approval for dolphin-safe tuna. Everyone recognizes those little dolphins on tuna cans.

FAIR TRADE: THE COFFEE CAMPAIGN

Coffee is one of the highest profile Fair Trade campaigns. And one of the bright spots for coffee farmers during these bleak times is the continued strength of the sustainable coffee market. Organic, shade-grown, and Fair Trade coffee all produce reasonable returns for the growers and these sustainable coffees have steadily increased their market share. A recent survey of retailers, wholesalers, roasters, and others involved in the coffee trade in North America concluded that 95 percent of the respondents thought that their sales of sustainable coffees were going to stay the same or increase. The estimated growth of sales of sustainable coffees was 27 percent, while 86 percent also thought that premiums for these coffees would continue in the future. The survey respondents represented the most knowledgeable players in the coffee market and it's telling that the vast majority of them viewed sustainable coffees as being a higher quality product with a robust future.

The largest obstacle hindering Fair Trade is a lack of availability. Consumer awareness is in its early stages and retailers have hesitated to stock Fair Trade products. A recent survey conducted by Anil Hira and Jared Ferrie at Simon Fraser University noted that Fair Trade certifiers have been reluctant to continue certifying new farms since there is an over-supply for their limited marketing lines given present demand. Still, the survey reveals a huge, and largely untapped, market for Fair Trade coffee.

Eight out of ten individuals interviewed believe companies should endorse a specific cause over a long period of time: 84 percent stated they perceive a company in a more positive light if it is contributing to making the world a better place; 78 percent of all adults questioned stated they would likely purchase a product linked with a cause they believe in; 66 percent said they would switch brands to support a cause they care about; 62 percent stated they would switch retail stores to support a cause; and 64 percent feel that cause-related marketing should be a regular component of a company's activities.

These numbers contrast with a more general survey of 1,487 coffee drinkers conducted by TransFair Canada in 2002, which found that only 11 percent were aware of Fair Trade coffee and that only four percent had purchased it. As the authors note, however, " many people are unaware of Fair Trade coffee, but once they understand what it entails, they are interested in purchasing it."[6]

TransFair USA, a nonprofit organization that certifies Fair Trade products, certified nine million pounds (4,050,000 kilograms) of Fair Trade coffee last year. This represents an increase of over 45 percent from the previous year. Today there are Fair Trade certification agencies all over the world, certifying crops such as coffee, bananas, and rice.

CHOCOLATE SLAVES

The International Cocoa Organization estimates that there are currently approximately 14 million people around the world directly involved in the annual production of 6 billion pounds (approximately 2.7 billion kilograms) of cocoa. While billions of dollars are made on an annual basis, very few producers receive prices that cover their costs of production or provide for a decent living. In fact, according to recent reports by the International Labor Organization (2001) and UNICEF (1998), low cocoa prices over the last five years have resulted in the enslavement of thousands of children in the production of cocoa on the Ivory Coast where most of the world's cocoa is grown.

Source: La Siembra website <www.lasiembra.com>.

BETTER BANANA PROJECT

Banana plantations have traditionally been seen as an ecological nightmare. Little regard has been given to the environmental impacts of banana farms in the past. Tropical rainforests contain almost 75 percent of the world's diversity in plants and animals, but unfortunately they are also excellent sites for banana plantations. The rapid expansion of banana plantations has led to widespread slash and burn deforestation, massive soil erosion and degradation, water contamination from soil and pesticide runoff, enormous amounts of waste primarily in the form of plastic bags, and endangerment of endemic species of flora and fauna. For every ton of bananas produced, two tons (1.8 metric tons) of waste are created. Plastic bags used on plantations have made it into the surrounding oceans, damaging reefs and killing sea turtles who mistake the bags for jellyfish. The average pesticide use in Costa Rica is 44 kilograms per hectare per year (97.02 pounds per 2.471 acres per year) — sixteen times the average pesticide use for crops in industrialized countries. Pesticides have been blamed for massive fish kills in rivers and have even been linked to the rapid decline of the coral reefs in Central and South America.

Banana plantations are also notorious for their unscrupulous abuse of workers' rights, from inadequate pay and long hours to poor safety standards and a general disregard for the well being of workers and their communities. The average Ecuadorian worker earns a dollar a day. Costa Rican plantation workers experience a pesticide poisoning rate of 6.4 percent, more than double the average pesticide poisoning rate for other agricultural workers in developing countries.

These were the issues that the Better Banana Project was created to address. The BBP is a banana certification program launched in 1991, designed to encourage the responsible production of bananas. The program was created by the Sustainable Agriculture Network (SAN), a coalition of non-profit conservation groups dedicated to promoting tropical conservation and encouraging the development of sustainable commercial agricultural practices. The Rainforest Alliance is the secretariat and lead agency of the group.

The average Canadian consumes 13 kilograms (28.9 pounds) of bananas a year. Worldwide exports of bananas totaled over 14 million tons (12.7 million metric tons), worth over $4 billion. Bananas are the fifth most important agricultural commodity in the world behind cereals, sugar, coffee, and cocoa. Almost 25 percent of the Gross Domestic Product of Ecuador and Costa Rica comes from the production of bananas. Only about 17 percent of the bananas produced in the world are exported; the rest are eaten locally. Brazil and India are two of the biggest producers in the world, but they don't export bananas.

In order to achieve certification, producers have to meet rigorous standards in regard to their commitment to the environment and to the local communities. Producers must satisfy a list of 256 criteria governing their operations, including:

- No deforestation of rainforests for new plantations is allowed, while lands not used for plantations must be reforested with native species.

- Water sources must be protected, with adequate buffers around rivers and pesticide and herbicide use regulated.
- Producers must ensure proper soil conservation, have recycling and composting facilities in place, and ensure and actively promote ecosystem and wildlife conservation.
- Workers must be paid fairly, receive proper benefits, work regulated hours, be provided with adequate housing, and be given adequate safety training and equipment. Hiring of workers should have no discrimination and no minors should be hired.
- Community development must be a company focus. (This primarily involves the active funding of community schools and training centers.)

Certification involves an initial visit by certification staff of the Sustainable Agriculture Network to outline the steps that must be undertaken by the producer to conform to the requirements. A second visit is conducted once the producer has initiated the required changes to determine if certification is in order. Once farms are certified, they're reassessed annually to ensure that they are still meeting the certification criteria. The Better Banana Project stresses that certification is not a goal, but a process. Farms are expected to make continuous improvements for their workers, their local communities, and the environment.

The Better Banana Project is now the largest banana certification program in the world. Over ten percent of the bananas produced in Latin America and the Caribbean are now certified by BBP. This represents over 160 farms and 120,000 hectares of plantations. One of the biggest players in the international banana market, Chiquita, announced in 2000 that 100 percent of the farms wholly owned by Chiquita were certified by the BBP, as well as 30 percent of the independent producers that supply Chiquita. The BBP has helped transform Chiquita into an industry leader in corporate social responsibility. Published in 2000, Chiquita's first CSR report was listed by SustainAbility, an international consulting firm specializing in business strategy and sustainable development, as one of the top 20 corporate responsibility reports released that year and the number one report in the food industry.

Reybancorp, the second largest banana producer in Ecuador, was the first company to certify 100 percent of its farms in 1999. Both Reybancorp and Chiquita have realized gains in productivity due to increased efficiencies and improved worker morale. Another great story that has emanated from the Better Banana Project is the success of Costa Rica's Agricultural College of the Humid Tropical Region. They own a large commercial operation on their grounds that received certification in 1994. The college and its students developed several imaginative techniques to reduce the use of agrochemicals and plastics and to manage wastes (including developing a process that turns banana-bunch stems into paper). Several of the innovations created by the college are part of the Better Banana Project standards and the school's graduates now spread their sustainable knowledge throughout the region.

RUGMARK: FREEING CHILDREN FROM BONDED LABOR

Raju was just seven years old when he was sold into bondage as a carpet weaver. His parents received the equivalent of around $50 from the Indian carpet loom owner for the indentured labor of their son. Raju spent the next year of his life working long hours every day weaving carpets in exchange for inadequate food and shelter, one of millions of children working in Southeast Asia. He was liberated from his servitude by RUGMARK inspectors and is now relishing the joys of learning at the Balashrya Center for Bonded Laborers in Badohi, India.

RUGMARK is a certification program focused on preventing the exploitation of children in the making of hand-knotted carpets and rugs in India, Pakistan, and Nepal. Indian activist Kailash Satyarthi had been trying to fight child labor for years when he decided that consumer pressure was the only way carpet makers would change their ways. Kailash is known worldwide for his fight against child labor, having personally emancipated some 28,000 children from bonded labor. The genesis of the RUGMARK Foundation came from Kailash, who in 1994 helped form a coalition of human rights organizations, companies exporting carpets from India, and UNICEF-India.

The program was first launched in Germany following a period of intense exposure that resulted from the efforts of human rights agencies and consumer advocates intent on informing the public about child labor in the manufacturing of carpets. The program certifies producers of carpets and rugs who are able to show that they are not using child labor in the manufacturing of their products. RUGMARK's quest to end child labor is done in concert with providing rehabilitation and schooling for former child weavers, ensuring that they have a brighter future.

Current estimates of child labor in the carpet industry in India, Nepal, and Pakistan are hard to get, due to the paucity of owners reporting child labor. However, the numbers are in the range of one to two million children, most of whom are in bonded servitude. These children face working days that can be up to 16 hours long, with few or no safety requirements. Children are abused, malnourished, robbed of their childhood, and are even at risk of death.

In order to qualify for the RUGMARK certification, carpet manufacturers must be able to prove that they utilize no child labor in their factories; they must register all of their looms with the RUGMARK Foundation; and they must consent to surprise inspections from RUGMARK inspectors. In exchange, producers can display the RUGMARK seal on their products, indicating to conscientious buyers that the carpet was made without the use of child labor.

The reality of life for many of these children is that if they are banned from working carpet looms, they will be forced into other forms of labor just as brutal or even worse. In Nepal, the majority of child workers are girls, and the risk is that they will be forced into prostitution if they can't support their families through carpet weaving. Thus the second mandate of the RUGMARK Foundation is to provide education and rehabilitation for the children they save from carpet factories. RUGMARK funds the creation and maintenance of schools and programs designed specifically for the children displaced by companies complying with RUGMARK standards. So far over 2,300 former child weavers have been given the opportunity to learn. The goal of RUGMARK is to reunite children with their families where possible, in which case RUGMARK provides support for school fees, books, uniforms, and other materials necessary for attending school. For every dollar spent on the development of a child, society will see a return of investment of seven dollars — thus the education of children is crucial to the vitality of developing countries.

To date over three million carpets have been certified with the RUGMARK label, with the amount of certified producers growing annually. RUGMARK inspectors save an average of three children every week. A 1997 UNICEF study found that 50 percent of the carpet weavers in Nepal were children; a follow-up study done two years later found that only five percent of workers were children, thanks to the work of RUGMARK. Unfortunately, there are still many carpet makers employing children and many more children are working in other industries, mainly the garment and agricultural industries. UNICEF estimates that there are probably 20 million child workers in the region and possibly as many as 40 million. The success of RUG-MARK may lead to certification programs for these other industries.

IKEA doesn't use the RUGMARK label, but it does certify that its rugs aren't made under sweatshop conditions. In 2000, IKEA provided US$ 500,000 in funding for a project aimed at preventing child labor in Uttar Pradesh, one of India's least developed states.

> ### Take A Stand Against Slavery
>
> *Before buying a hand-knotted rug, ask your retailer if they have a policy regarding the labor practices of their suppliers. Buying a Fair Trade rug not only financially supports the rights of workers, but encourages retailers to continue to support them. It sends a message that you, the consumer, are not willing to tolerate slave labor.*

MARINE STEWARDSHIP COUNCIL

In Canada, the closing of the cod fishery on the East Coast is a vivid example of a fishery that has been over exploited to the point of severe depletion. The ecological impacts are yet to be understood, but the communities that depend on fishing for their livelihood feel the economic impact of shutting down a fishery immediately. The turmoil caused by the collapse of the Northern Atlantic cod stocks highlights the importance of creating sustainable fisheries for the benefit of everyone.

The cod stocks of the Grand Banks have been one of the richest fishing areas in the world for the last 500 years, and arguably one of the cornerstones in the creation of Canada, as we know it. Between 1850 and 1950, the northern cod catch grew from about 200,000 metric tons (220,400 short tons) to around 300,000 metric tons (330,600 short tons). With the advent of new technology, modern factory ships can haul in as much cod in an hour as a typical sixteenth century fishing boat could land in an entire season (around 100 metric tons or 110.2 short tons). After the introduction of massive new fishing trawlers, the annual catch shot up to around 800,000 metric tons (881,600 short tons), which lasted until the mid-seventies when the fishery underwent a sudden drop. The cod stocks have rebounded a couple of times, but never to the same extent as their original levels and have now almost vanished.[7]

The Marine Stewardship Council (MSC) was created as a means of promoting sustainable fish harvesting management throughout the world. By creating a certification label, they hope to harness the power of the consumer in nudging the world's fisheries towards a sustainable approach to their business. The MSC was created in 1996 through the unique partnership of food industry giant Unilever and the World Wildlife Fund (WWF). Unilever's interests were both altruistic, to protect and preserve marine ecosystems, and commercial, to ensure a reliable source of seafood through a sustainable fishery. The MSC became wholly independent of Unilever and the World Wildlife Fund in 1999, ensuring its impartiality as an organization removed from industry influence.

The MSC strives to bring a holistic management of fisheries that provides long-term sustainability both economically and ecologically. The accreditation process requires fisheries to apply for certification, whereupon a third party certifier accredited by the MSC does an audit of the management of the fishery to determine if it meets the principles and criteria of the MSC. Once certified, the fishery can display the MSC label on their products. Every five years the fishery must go through the entire certification process again to ensure that they are still meeting the criteria. The basic premise of the certification program can be boiled down to the following points. The fishery must:

- Be able to continue indefinitely at a reasonable level.
- Maintain and promote ecological health and abundance, protecting diversity and quality of habitat.
- Be managed in a responsible manner that adheres to all local, national, and international laws and regulations.
- Be able to maintain current and future economic and social benefits to the local stakeholders.
- Be conducted in a socially and economically fair and responsible manner.

There are currently seven fisheries that have been certified by the MSC; several more have applied and are going through the certification process. The Western Australian rock lobster fishery was the first fishery to be certified by the MSC in 2000. The Western Australian rock lobster fishery represents about 20 percent of the total value of Australia's fisheries. The fishery was recognized for its strict adherence to sustainable harvests since the 1960's. The accreditation process took 15 months, which is about the standard time involved to achieve certification. The Alaska salmon fishery was also certified in 2000, while the BC salmon fishery is currently going through the accreditation process for Marine Stewardship Council certification.

The Marine Stewardship Council also promotes stores that stock MSC certified fishery products, and their website gives the details about where to buy MSC certified goods. This is in line with their goal of strengthening the entire chain of custody for fishery goods, from the fishing boats to the processing plant to the supermarket.[8]

THE NEW GREEN CONSUMER

In a 1999 poll, 51 percent of respondents from North America and Oceania reported that they had punished a company perceived as not behaving responsibly by speaking out against it or consciously avoiding its products.[9] And according to a 2000 Mori poll, 70 percent of European consumers said that a company's commitment to social responsibility is important when buying a product or service, and 20 percent would be very willing to pay more for products that are socially and environmentally responsible.

Not everyone who answers positively goes out and buys green every time, of course. Market researchers know that you have to discount such figures to get at a true measure of buying behavior. According to Roper ASW's "Green Gauge" survey, 15 percent of the American public is very likely to back up their green sensibilities with their purchasing decisions. But since these green market segments also tend to be more highly educated and more affluent and concentrated in metropolitan areas they are attractive from a marketing perspective. Fifty-one percent of consumers don't need to go green to entice companies to start producing for the green marketplace!

We *are* willing to pay more for products that are more environmentally friendly than competing products. The key, however, is that willingness to pay is often linked not to a general environmental halo around the product, but to an identifiable benefit to the consumer. Organic food, which is sold on the basis of both environmental and health benefits commands a premium in the marketplace — and is growing rapidly. Worldwide sales of organic products are estimated at US$20 billion. Canadian organic retail sales growth is expected to increase 20 per cent a year to Can$3.1 billion in 2005 (according to Agriculture and Agri-Food Canada).

Part of the problem has been that consumers don't always feel that they have all the facts, and sometimes feel that searching out green products is too inconvenient. Research has shown that 44 percent of Americans say they would try harder to purchase green products if environmentally friendly products were readily available to them.[10]

A SHOPPER'S EXPERIENCE

Even if you have a lot of information, it still isn't easy to be a responsible consumer, especially when there isn't a certification process or seal of approval available. Suppose you need new running shoes. Seems like it would be a simple consumer choice doesn't it. But after researching the subject, we realized that buying running shoes is anything but simple — unless being a vegan is your only concern. (I know that seems like a non sequitur but read on!) If you want to buy shoes that haven't been made in a sweatshop under atrocious working conditions, then — good luck!

Almost all of the big shoe companies do at least some of their manufacturing in Indonesia or China and have questionable labor practices. Some, like adidas-Salomon, Reebok, and Nike have written policies but are still lagging in actual practices. Reebok and adidas-Salomon are further along the curve than most in terms of transparency around their offshore operations, and adidas-Saloman has boycotted Indian leather over gross mistreatment of animals in the Indian leather trade.

When we researched this, a number of people recommended New Balance or Saucony shoes because they're made in the US. And while you can find the odd model that's been made in North America by fairly paid workers, neither company has a written policy about their foreign suppliers and their foreign (mainly Chinese) factories. So you may still be supporting sweatshops when you buy a "Made In USA" shoe from them. There are a few small shops in the US who make all of their shoes in the US. Simple and Vans are probably the largest ones with good distribution.

We were excited to find that some manufacturers make shoes with recycled materials. We were disappointed to find that, other than .Simple, most of these brands aren't readily available. The waters are further muddied by smaller distributors that advertise vegan or vegetarian shoes that sound great and may even taste great but might have been made in a sweatshop. Argh! To help bring some clarity to the subject I interviewed Heather White, the founder and executive director of Verité.

INSIDE THE SWEATSHOPS: WHO MAKES YOUR SHOES?

Deb Abbey: Tell me a little bit about Verité, Heather.

Heather White: Verité's mission is to ensure that people world-wide work under safe, fair, and legal conditions through independent monitoring of factories, education, and training. We link with nonprofit and human rights organizations to interview workers off-site and bring their voices and experiences into the process of identifying workplace violations and improving factory conditions.

DA: Let's start with the company that's been the highest-profile target of the anti-sweatshop campaign. What do you think of Nike?

HW: The campaigns that have been targeting Nike for the last several years have built a good information gathering network and have been effective in making their concerns public. The grassroots groups have been accurate in identifying serious issues in Nike factories in Asia and Latin America. Verité has visited many Nike factories, usually on behalf of other companies, and through our process of information gathering over a two-week period, we have documented similar concerns. With the Kukdong case and the Global Alliance report, it appears that, when criticized publicly, Nike is making progress on how the company addresses those concerns and is making improvements.

DA: Which companies are behaving most responsibly?

HW: Several companies are now investing quite heavily in programs to improve factory working conditions and placing information in the hands of workers. Notable among these are Timberland, adidas-Salomon, and Reebok. New Balance's program

is interesting because it is managed directly by the head of production for the company, who has close relationships with each of
their factories and is able to use significant pressure to encourage
suppliers to make the improvements the company wants.

DA: What should responsible consumers demand of the companies in this sector?

HW: They should regularly call the toll-free numbers and send
letters to the companies asking them direct questions about
what is being done to ensure that children are not employed in
their factories and that working conditions are safe and healthy
and in legal compliance. Shareholders should vote their proxies
at a company's annual general meeting if there is a resolution on
supplier standards or sweatshop issues.

To make your voice heard by the shoe companies, contact
them directly.

adidas America
5055 N. Greely Ave.
Portland, OR 97217
Attn: Consumer Relations
E-mail:Consumer.Relations@adidasus.com.
Website: www.adidas.com
Phone: 1-800-448-1796

Nike Canada Limited
Head Office
175 Commerce Valley Drive West, Suite 500
Thornhill, ON L3T 7P6
Website: www.nike.com
Phone: 1-800-663-6453

Nike USA
One Bowerman Drive
Beaverton, Oregon 97005-6453
Website: www.nike.com
Phone: (503) 641-6453

Reebok International Ltd.
PO Box 1060
Ronks, PA 17573
Website: www.reebok.com
Phone: 1-800-843-4444

New Balance Athletic Shoe, Inc.
Brighton Landing
20 Guest Street
Boston, MA 02135-2088
Website: www.nbwebexpress.com
Phone: 1-800-253-7463

Saucony, Inc.
13 Centennial Drive
Peabody, MA 01961
Website: www.saucony.com
Phone: 1-800-365-4933

Simple – USA
495–A South Fairview Avenue
Goleta, California 93117
E-mail: info@simpleshoes.com
Phone: 1-888-432-8530

VANS
15700 Shoemaker Avenue
Santa Fe Springs, CA 90670 – 5515
Website: www.vans.com
Phone: 1-800-826-7800

ARE WE BUYING GREEN?

The Co-operative Bank in the UK has done the most extensive tracking of the ethical market and since 1999 has been producing the Ethical Purchasing Index (EPI). The EPI is the bank's attempt to measure growth in the marketplace for ethical goods and services. The data they gather is specific to the UK, but the strength of the trends they have discovered indicates the growth of ethical goods and services is probably a trend that holds true for North America to some degree.

The EPI shows that ethical consumption in the UK grew by £1.1 billion in 2001, increasing the total value of ethical purchasing to £6.8 billion, a total growth of 19 percent. The overall market share of ethical goods grew by nine percent. Including money deposited in ethical banks and in ethical investments, the total value of the ethical marketplace in 2001 was £13.9 billion. All of the sectors of the green market showed growth in 2001. Sales of green energy was the fastest growing sector of the market, increasing market share by 125 percent. Organics grew by 28 percent while the sales of Fair Trade teas and coffees grew by just under 35 percent.

The authors of the Ethical Purchasing Index state that eco-labeling does work and is in part responsible for the growth of ethical consumerism. Household items, such as energy efficient appliances, now comprise almost 60 percent of the market, due in large part to the success of eco-labeling schemes.

The organic industry has shown an annual growth rate of over 20 percent in Canada, the US, and the UK. In the US alone, sales are expected to hit $20 billion by 2005 while reaching 40 percent of US households.[11] It is worth noting that the industry has shown such rapid growth in the absence of the big players (i.e., the "name brands"). Once the mainstream players jump into the market, the growth could be significant.

The Lifestyles of Health and Sustainability (LOHAS) market in the US is represented by 63 million Americans, which translates into a $226.8 billion market. Worldwide, the market for LOHAS products is estimated at $546 billion, according to the Natural Marketing Institute. LOHAS consumers are more likely to choose environment friendly products and are willing to pay more for sustainable products.

IDEALSWORK

> The European Union has committed to reaching a target of 22.1 percent of all energy coming from renewable sources by 2010.
>
> — www.IdealsWork.com

The complexity of making consumer choices that matter is what makes a company like IdealsWork.com so exciting. Think of Amazon.com meets Ben & Jerry's — an Internet shopping engine that is trying to change the world as well as to make money.

IdealsWork.com's search engine provides consumers with ratings of thousands of brands, personalized according to their individual concerns and value preferences. Consumers can compare the social and environmental performance of thousands of product brands — using criteria they select and weight according to their own preferences — on issues that include the environment, diversity, labor practices, women's issues, human rights and treatment of animals. After comparing companies' social and environmental ratings, IdealsWork.com users can purchase a refrigerator from company A, and if they choose, send a message to company B notifying it that it just lost a customer due to, say, it's environmental record.

Each purchase made through IdealsWork.com also supports worthy charities and non-profits. IdealsWork.com is trying to make it financially beneficial for companies to improve their social and environmental practices — because consumers will reward those companies with increased sales. Companies with problematic records will see a cost when consumers avoid their products and do business with their competitors instead. In other words, the team at IdealsWork.com are trying to eliminate the choice businesses face between doing the right thing and doing the profitable thing — by making them one and the same.

Consumer pressure needs to be complemented by collective action to effect change. But consumers have to step up to the plate once products are on the market or companies won't stay committed. The IdealsWork website captures the essence of pro-active consumerism:

> No matter which issues you care about, chances are that companies have a lot to do with them. Changing the practices of companies is a key to building a brighter future. And as powerful as companies are, there's something even more powerful: you.
>
> Companies do what customers want. In fact, the main reason companies have not been more environmentally and socially responsible is because customers haven't demanded it.[12]

USING YOUR MONEY FOR SOCIAL CHANGE

Co-op America is an American non-profit organization that has been educating individuals and businesses about responsible consumerism since 1982. Co-op America operates under the philosophy that individuals can use their economic power to influence positive change in society, while businesses that care about community, Fair Trade, and the environment should be encouraged to succeed and grow. With nearly 50,000 individual members and 2,000 business members, Co-op America has styled itself as a one-stop shop for empowering individuals and businesses to use their economic clout for social change. Co-op America runs a family of websites that cover the wide range of issues that encompass economic activism.

- **www.coopamerica.org** Powerful steps for using your consumer and investor power for social change.
- **www.responsibleshopper.org** Provides consumers with information about the social and environmental performance of companies, brands and products. The site is intended to empower the consumer to make ethical decisions.

- **www.greenpages.org** An on-line directory of socially and environmentally responsible companies that have been screened by Co-op America

- **www.sweatshops.org** Dedicated to increasing the Fair Trade market share and ending sweatshop labor. Provides information on the leaders in the field and gives tips on how to encourage other companies to follow suit.

- **www.woodwise.org** Dedicated to the conservation of our forests through the responsible use of paper and wood products. Lists tips for activism and names those products and companies that are doing the most to encourage responsible forest stewardship.

- **www.boycotts.org** Lists current boycotts and explains their origins. It also gives tips on how to start your own boycotts.

- **www.communityinvest.org** Promotes financing that creates resources and opportunities for economically disadvantaged individuals that have been traditionally underserved by financial institutions — responsible banking.

- **www.socialinvest.org** Designed to educate the ethical investor. Information, contacts, and resources about ethical investing and ethical funds.

- **www.realmoney.org** Provides people with practical information on how to live a greener lifestyle, from which funds to invest in to what kind of products to buy.

- **www.shareholderaction.org** A clearinghouse of information on shareholder advocacy. Strives to link the various facets of the socially responsible investment community, from financial advisors to environmental organizations, to empower effective shareholder activism.

HELP! ADVICE FOR THE CARING CONSUMER

It's not enough to avoid the companies and products that you don't like. Boycotting is useful but it's not enough. Certification is useful but not available for all product areas. Be proactive and deal with companies that are part of the solution. Contact companies and let them know that you're not interested in products that support environmental degradation or human rights abuses or other abhorrent practices. Contact companies and let them know that you will buy products that are environmentally friendly and socially sustainable. Contact companies and let them know that you care about how they treat their employees and customers and suppliers and the communities where they operate. For contact information, see the Resources section at the end of this book.

Pension 7 Power

I F YOU FEEL POWERLESS reading about shareholder activism because your retirement funds are locked up in a pension plan — don't.

As a member of a pension plan, you are a shareholder in the companies in which the plan invests. Your pension plan buys shares on your behalf with contributions made by you and your employer. When people plan for retirement, they're usually more worried about whether they will have enough to live on than about what business activities their retirement savings are supporting. That's understandable — no one wants to retire broke! But retirees need more than a monthly check to live in comfort. They also need clean air and water, a stable and peaceful world, and a well-governed society.

Pension plans are some of the most important players in today's increasingly global financial markets, and individuals can make a difference. You can help mobilize your pension savings to promote the kind of world you want to retire in and provide the returns necessary for financial security. Showing an interest in your plan helps ensure that the trustees, investment managers, and administrators are accountable to you, the beneficiary.

Pension fund activism has been made possible by the incredible growth of pension funds over the last 50 years. I wonder if anyone really thought that the workers would own the means of production. The numbers tell the story.

In 1950, pension funds accounted for less than one percent of publicly traded equity in the USA. By 2001, they owned 45 percent of publicly traded equity.[1] In the US, pension fund managers are less inhibited by regulations that limit the amount of stock an institutional investor can own, so they can buy massive blocks of stock that allow pension funds to bend the ear of corporations. Pension funds can exert a lot more influence over corporations than individual investors can on their own. In Canada, the total assets of trusteed plans have grown from $4 billion in 1961 to $543.8 billion at the end of 2002, the second largest pool of investment capital after the chartered banks.[2]

Pension funds in the US didn't become shareholder activists until the mid-eighties. That year saw the filing of numerous proxies from large funds such as the California Public Employees' Retirement System (CalPERS) and the New York City funds. In fact, almost 20 percent of all shareholder proposals filed in 1986 came from just five pension funds.

The increase in activism closely followed the creation of the Council of Institutional Investors (CII) in 1985. The CII, which consists primarily of pension funds, was created in response to questionable takeover activities that pension fund trustees felt would have negative impacts on their beneficiaries. One of the initial founders of the CII was CalPERS. The fund had witnessed an objectionable stock transaction between Texaco and major shareholders who were threatening a takeover. Texaco, a large CalPERS holding, essentially paid off the shareholders in order to save management positions that were in jeopardy in the event of a takeover. This marked the beginning of active involvement in shareholder proxies by pension funds.

In the beginning, the focus of pension fund activism was on corporate governance issues, severance packages, poison pill policies, CEO pay, and so on. Pension funds that were heavily indexed (invested in indices such as the Standard and Poor 500) — as CalPERS was — often hoped to influence the greater market through the targeting of individual companies. Their philosophy was that companies would want to avoid the bad publicity involved with the filing of a proposal and would therefore be proactive about the issues that CalPERS was pushing, the majority of which were designed to increase the profitability of the companies. These efforts seem to have been successful. A Wilshire Associates study of the "CalPERS Effect" of corporate governance activities examined the performance of 95 companies highlighted on CalPERS' annual target list between 1987 and 1999. Results indicated that while the stock of these companies trailed the Standard & Poor's 500 Index by 96 percent in the five-year period before CalPERS acted, the same stocks outperformed the index by 14 percent in the following five years, adding almost US$150 million in additional returns to the fund.[3] In the words of Richard Koppes, former chief counsel of CalPERS, "It makes sense for us to try to raise the ocean in order to lift our boat."[4]

Pension fund activism was not directed solely at corporate governance, although the majority of activism was. There are a few examples of shareholder proposals relating to social content. In 1987, the New York State Common Retirement Fund began what became a wave of shareholder activism asking companies to completely withdraw from doing business in South Africa. The fund's action lent the kind of muscle that shareholder activists were hoping for in the fight to force companies into socially responsible positions. Altogether, 156 South Africa resolutions were filed for the spring proxy season, more than the number of social policy resolutions on all issues that had come to votes the previous year. Of those, proponents withdrew 45 of the proposals once companies agreed to leave South Africa. The 63 proposals that came to votes received an average of 12.2 percent support. Between 1986 and 1989, 136 companies had cut their direct investment links with South Africa.

By combining their assets, pension funds like CalPERS and the New York State Common Retirement Fund can bring enormous pressure on companies. Together the two funds alone have more than $230 billion in assets.

Religious groups have also been prominent filers of social issue proposals and have had a major impact on the development of shareholder activism. The General Board of Pension and Health Benefits, the pension fund run in the interests of the United Methodist Church and its congregation, is the largest pension fund operated by a religious denomination, with more than $11 billion in its portfolio.

The board is very active in using its financial clout to address social issues. They file about 25 resolutions a year, and usually end up withdrawing about half of them when companies agree to address their concerns. The fund has managed to develop relationships with large companies such as Wal-Mart and Nike as a direct result of their shareholder proposals. They feel that being able to garner an audience with these large companies is much more efficient than attacking from outside the company walls.

NYCER Approach Yields Results

The New York City Employees Retirement System (NYCERS) has been a leader in the filing of proposals that seek to ban workplace discrimination based on sexual orientation. NYCERS has created significant publicity in their fight to get ExxonMobil to adapt their hiring policies. Their most recent proposal gathered 27.1 percent of ExxonMobil shares, an increase of 15 percent over the previous year's proxy vote.

I recently had the great pleasure of meeting Pat Doherty, the senior manager of social responsibility in the New York City Comptroller's office. Pat has been involved in shareholder campaigns on behalf of New York City (NYC) since the mid-eighties, when local citizens approached NYC about South African divestment and the Global Sullivan Principles. With Northern Ireland front and center in the news, it became apparent that they also needed a set of principles for companies operating there. Since Pat was the Irish guy on the team, he was asked to draft them. They became the McBride Principles. Since then, two-thirds of the companies in the NYC pension plans have adopted those principles.

Pat and I share some strong opinions about strategies for shareholder activism. At NYC they start the process by writing to the company to let them know that they're filing a shareholder proposal. This gives the company an opportunity to comply with the proposal and that's always a win-win for the shareholder (in this case NYC) and for the company. But companies don't always agree with the direction outlined in the proposal, and in that case the proposal goes to the vote at the company's annual general meeting.

Moving Companies in the Right Direction

Pat is very clear about NYC's role as a shareholder. They maintain good relationships with the companies in their portfolio. They're not trying to destroy the companies. In some cases they might have a billion dollars invested in a company. They're looking for an outcome that moves the company in the right direction and preserves shareholder value. All of the issues that they deal with are bottom line issues. He believes that they have helped many of the companies that they own.

Pat doesn't usually withdraw a resolution in exchange for structured dialogue with a company. He says:

"It's not a case of educating them and it's not a case of convincing them. They're smart people. If they're ready to move, these discussions can be very quick. It can be a couple of 20 minute conversations. If they're not ready to move then no amount of dialogue will get them there. The people in these corporations work for us, the shareholders — we own the company. Dialogue about these issues is a right, not something we should have to barter or trade for.

"If the company says 'We can't do this, we can't do that,' then we say, 'Okay, we'll see you at the next annual meeting.' We don't go away; we just file and re-file. We end up getting a lot of agreements because they know that we're not going away.

"There have been times when we've had reasonable arguments from companies and we can accommodate that. On the sexual orientation issue, we've been very successful in getting companies to agree to develop policies against discrimination. A number of companies thought that they would be inundated with lawsuits. We pulled out the statistics and showed them that they were not going to get a mountain of lawsuits unless they were involved in egregious practices."

Defeating Human Rights Abuses in West Papua

One of Pat's favorite shareholder activism success stories is actually an example of a technical defeat. The company is Freeport-

McMoRan, a gold and copper mining company that owns the largest gold mine in the world in West Papua, Indonesia. The company boasts that it has produced exceptionally high volumes at low costs — and it claims to be dedicated to human rights and asserts it has engaged in consultation with the local community regarding its operational impact in West Papua.

According to the International Right to Know Campaign, the reality is very different. The company wrote its own contract with the Indonesian government. And a sweetheart deal it was, providing sweeping powers over the local population, including the right to confiscate any natural resources without paying taxes or compensating the indigenous population. Villagers have been forcibly relocated and barred from lands controlled by the company. Tactics such as bombing and bulldozing were used to clear out the locals.

In Pat's words:

"Human rights people from Papua visited us. And then in August 2002, several American teachers that were teaching Freeport-McMoRan employees were ambushed and slaughtered on their way back from a picnic. The Indonesian military said that this was the work of West Papua rebels. Well, it turned out that it was the military that had ambushed and killed the employees. We went to the company and said, 'You're giving a lot of money to the military and they're killing your employees. The bribes that you're paying contravene the Foreign Corrupt Practices Act.' The Robert F. Kennedy Center in Washington had issued a report in July 2002 in which they had made some recommendations to the company. "We brought a resolution to Freeport-McMoRan asking the company to improve its international social and human rights policy. In particular, we wanted more information about Freeport's relationship with the Indonesian army in Papua. Shareholders have a right to know more about what companies like Freeport are doing overseas.

"The company contested our resolution at the US Securities and Exchange Commission. They had adopted some of the Robert F. Kennedy Center's amendments without fanfare.

Freeport had also sent us documents outlining how much they were paying the military. They told the SEC that not only had they adopted some of the amendments but also that they had released these documents to us. We didn't release the documents, since we received them on a confidential basis, but the Securities and Exchange Commission made them public and it caused a huge furor in Indonesia. The payments hadn't been made public before and the government wasn't happy. This led to a very significant movement to curtail the military from making agreements with foreign companies."

The report revealed that Freeport-McMoRan paid 4.7 million dollars in "protection money" to the military in 2001 and an additional 5.6 million dollars in 2002. Not everyone in the military was happy, either. Freeport-McMoRan indicated that the money was intended for housing and other services for soldiers in order to minimize conflict with the local population. Nonetheless, it appears that most of the money stayed in the hands of the ranking military officers, and there was discontent among the grassroots soldiers.

The Securities and Exchange Commission allowed Freeport to omit the shareholder resolution because they had already complied with part of the resolution, including the disclosure of funds supplied to the Indonesian military. This is a case in which a shareholder proposal didn't succeed — but by trying to exclude it, the company exposed itself to scrutiny from all sides. So Freeport-McMoRan can count on seeing another resolution from the NYC, and another and another, for as long as it takes.

Battling Discrimination in the Cracker Barrel Case

Another major success for NYC was the sexual orientation campaign with Cracker Barrel-Old Country Stores. With a name like Cracker Barrel, the company had a down-home Southern image to maintain. Ten years ago, their vice-president of human resources sent out the following memo: "It is inconsistent with our concept and values, and is perceived to be inconsistent with those of our customer base, to continue to employ individuals in our operating units whose sexual preferences fail to demonstrate normal heterosexual values which have been the foundation of families in our society."

Eleven employees lost their jobs as a result of the policy. One worker received a pink slip stating, "This employee is being terminated due to violation of company policy.... The employee is gay."

The company retracted the policy but refused to exclude sexual orientation discrimination. In 1992, NYC filed a shareholder resolution asking the company to include sexual orientation in its Equal Employment Opportunity (EEO) policies. The resolution failed because Cracker Barrel persuaded the Securities and Exchange Commission that the resolution could be omitted from its proxy because it was categorized as "ordinary business." The Securities and Exchange Commission used this ruling as something of a precedent and the *Cracker Barrel Rule* was used to treat all such shareholder resolutions as ordinary business.

In 1993 NYC sued the Securities and Exchange Commission to have the decision overturned on the grounds that the commission had neglected to solicit public comment and that it had irrationally reversed long-standing policy without adequate justification. The court ruled in favor of the Securities and Exchange Commission's right to issue no-action clauses as it saw fit, because they were not legally binding and proponents could sue companies in court to obtain access to the proxy ballot. Finally, in 1998, the Securities and Exchange Commission announced that it would no longer back companies that wanted to exclude shareholder resolutions that addressed discrimination issues.

During this time, NYC just kept going back to the company year after year. Finally, after ten years, they got 58 percent of the vote at the AGM and the board of directors voted immediately to unanimously amend its Equal Employment Opportunities policy to include protection against sexual orientation discrimination. NYC just wore them down. Every year for ten years, they got more and more votes.

Campaigning on Many Fronts

This was the first time a North American social content resolution received a majority of the vote when management was opposed.

After the vote, NYCERS got several other big companies to agree to the same resolution. If they're putting out a resolution on a specific topic, all the companies get virtually the same resolution. In direct response to pressure from NYC, J.C. Penney, TXU Corporation, Ingram Micro, American Electric Power, and Dynegy Inc., all moved to explicitly bar discrimination based on sexual orientation before putting the proposals to vote. The fund withdrew its proposals in acknowledgment of the companies' action.[5]

A lot of social investors approach specific companies with very specific issues. Pat Doherty thinks that there are a lot of things that all companies should do and will benefit from. Whether it's the International Labor Organization standards, independent monitoring, sexual orientation, or any number of other issues, he believes that all companies will benefit from adopting these policies.

Going forward, NYC will be dealing with lots of corporate governance issues. They're especially interested in the ability of stockholders to put opposing director candidates on the ballot without having to spend millions to get them there. This will greatly improve corporate democracy and act as a check against some of the worst Enron-type abuses. They're also interested in getting companies to follow through on issues that the majority of shareholders think are important. If management decides that it's not in the best interest of the company then they may decide not to adopt the resolution.

NYC will continue to work on several ongoing campaigns. They're active in anti-sweatshop and anti-discrimination in employment, and they promote Global Reporting Initiative and sexual orientation campaigns. They start at the top of the Fortune 500 companies and then just keep going down the list. Many of the companies they file with agree to do what they ask. Last year, NYCERS negotiated withdrawal from 16 shareholder proposals.

NYC's approach has evolved over the past two decades. Pat says that they're more likely to join with other stakeholders and shareholders in cosponsoring a resolution. Out of 80 to 85 resolutions they filed this past year, they cosponsored ten. They can bring their significant shareholdings to the table as clout and help out others, while extending the reach of their own campaigns. For instance, in their sweatshop campaigns they're working with trade union shareholders and religious organizations and NGOs overseas, especially in China, Indonesia, and Viet Nam.

The New York State Common Retirement Funds is the second largest pension fund in the US and it was very active filing proposals relating to environmental responsibility in 2003. Last year the fund filed proposals with General Electric (GE) and Kodak, asking them to address the environmental ramifications of their business. In GE's case, the fund wants the company to divulge the amount of money the company is spending dealing with PCB contamination issues, while Kodak has been asked to reduce its use of environmentally-damaging chemicals.

Pension Reform, UK-style

In July of 2000, the British government issued the Socially Responsible Investment Regulation, which requires pension fund trustees to disclose their policies on socially responsible investment, including shareholder activism. As a result, pension funds have become increasingly active in addressing social and environmental criteria in regard to their holdings.

A recent survey of 101 trustees of pension funds in the UK indicated a growing emphasis on social responsibility through stock selection and shareholder activism. Of the trustees interviewed, 69 percent already took into account social, ethical, and environmental performance issues when selecting stocks. Thirty-seven percent of trustees thought that pension fund activism would result in substantial improvements in corporate social responsibility within the next ten years, while another 48 percent thought that there would be some improvements. Pension funds in the UK represent around a third of all market investments in the UK.[6]

Proxy Voting

In Canada, shareholder activism has been much more restricted by the regulatory environment. Until recently, the Canada Business Corporations Act (CBCA) allowed management to reject proposals that they felt promoted general economic, political, racial, or social causes. As a result, Canadian companies were able to restrict the growth of shareholder activism in Canada. In addition, most pension funds in Canada have adopted rather conservative views on their fiduciary responsibilities and as a result are less involved with shareholder activism than their counterparts in the US. This was evident in a survey of pension fund investment managers in Canada by the Shareholder Association for Research and Education (SHARE), asking how they voted on certain proxy proposals. They found that 90 percent of the voting is done at the managers' discretion. That is, the investment managers (rather than the pension funds) decide how to vote on the vast number of proxies that are brought to the vote. Twenty-five of the firms polled said that they had discretion to vote on 98 percent of proposals.

Stephen Viederman, the founder and director of the Initiative for Fiduciary Responsibility (IFR) and former president of the Jessie Smith Noyes Foundation believes that fiduciaries must take responsibility for voting proxies on behalf of the plan beneficiaries. In a speech given in 2002, he stated that:

> Fiduciary responsibility requires the voting of proxies on shareholder resolutions relating to issues of corporate governance and social concerns. Proxies are assets to be exercised in beneficiaries' interest. This is not an argument that there is a "right" way to vote on corporate governance and social issues, where differences can legitimately exist. Many shareholder resolutions can be correlated with increased shareholder value, especially with consumer-oriented companies. What is obvious, however, is that not voting proxies or voting blindly with management is a squandering of assets....
>
> Fiduciaries should develop proxy-voting guidelines, make them available to their beneficiaries, and disclose their actual votes on proxy resolutions. Fiduciaries are the stewards of capital entrusted to them to look out for all their beneficiary interests.[7]

Fiduciary responsibility is a complex legal issue so we asked Gil Yaron to clarify it for us. Gil is a lawyer specializing in the subject of fiduciary duties as they apply to pension trustees, and author of *The Responsible Trustee*.

Reluctance felt by pension trustees about socially responsible investing comes from concerns about breaching their fiduciary duties. A fiduciary relationship exists where one person puts their trust and reliance in another person. Pension trustees are one example of fiduciaries. As fiduciaries, pension trustees are required by law to act with the care, skill and diligence of a reasonable person when handling pension assets. They also have to act in the best interests of pension plan members and beneficiaries and treat them with an even hand.

Many argue that investing in a socially responsible manner breaches these fiduciary responsibilities. However, this view is too vague. When people talk about social investing, they usually think only of investment screens (e.g. no tobacco, military, nuclear, etc.). In fact, social investment includes three elements — shareholder activism, proxy voting, and investment screening — and the law treats them all differently. Proxies are considered a valuable plan asset and must be voted by all pension plans. Shareholder activism is merely an extension of proxy voting and the democratic involvement of shareholders in corporate governance. Investment screening is a little more problematic. Debate has raged about the ability of fiduciaries to apply social and environmental screens to investments for a number of reasons. While the issue is not resolved, there is an increasing body of legal and empirical evidence supporting the use of investment screening. More and more people now recognize that investment screening can be part of a prudent investment selection process, provided it is well researched and monitored and consistent with the pension plan's investment policy.[8]

How To for Pension Trustees

Darcie Beggs, the Senior Research Officer, Pension and Benefits at the Canadian Union of Public Employees (CUPE) is a stalwart. I trust her to make sure that the beneficiaries of any plan that she's involved in have a better world in which to retire. I asked Darcie why pension plans are turning to shareholder activism.

Darcie Beggs: I can't answer for all plans but in the case of CUPE member pension plans, the union decided in 1989 to make pensions a priority. We began focusing on gaining joint trusteeship of the larger multi-employer/multi-union plans (given their nature we couldn't really bargain) as a means of having a real say over the plans and funds. Shareholder activism is a logical outcome of worker control and ensuring that our members deferred wages work in the interests of working people and their communities. This is about putting trade union principles to work.

Deb Abbey: What are the main challenges for pension trustees who want to address social and environmental issues in the investment decision making process?

DB: I would say the "suits." The pension investment industry and the consultants that promote that the only job of the trustee is to maximize profits regardless of the consequences. They ask trade unionists to leave their union hats at the door, when clearly they can't do that. We haven't had enough information, until recently, to fight the status quo.

DA: Do you have advice for a new pension trustee who wants to get active?

DB: Talk to other union trustees. Take trade union based trustee training. Remember you are the trustee, so keep asking questions so that you can make informed decisions. The service providers must speak to you in your language. Don't be embarrassed about asking the same question over and over until you are comfortable making a decision. Seek lots of information.

DA: What about advice for a plan beneficiary who wants their plan to be more active?

DB: The fund is yours. It's trust property that is to work in the best interest of the plan members. As a member, you should expect that those responsible will represent you. You should make your views known. Ensure that the union is also voicing an opinion to those responsible. Ask for information, like the portfolio holdings, how proxies were voted, etc.

DA: What factors are critical for effective social impact investing by pension plans?

DB: Informed trustees, an active membership, service providers that are encouraging, good sources of information.

DA: Where do you think we'll be in ten years' time?

DB: Who knows, but I am hopeful that we'll have legislation that requires plans to take socially responsible investing into account. More of our pension plans will be trusteed by trade unionists that will ensure investment policies require investing with trade union principles. I am also hopeful that we will have legislation that requires pension plan service providers to have a fiduciary duty to plan members. I think this will change the outlook a lot.

DA: What is the role of organized labor in pressing for more social involvement on the part of jointly-trusteed plans?

DB: In the public sector, and CUPE in particular, we have made gaining joint trusteeship (union and employer), a priority. We have had success. I think that because of this success that we have pushed the industry to take on investment issues using a trade union principled view. The labor movement must continue to provide information, education, and other resources to our pension trustees to help them do their jobs as trustees. It can be lonely work. We also need to continue to lobby governments to change laws that enable investing with union principles easier. We must continue to meet with the Canadian Institute of Actuaries, investment professionals, and others, to make them aware of our concerns.

DA: Do you have any advice for pension committees in terms of encouraging mainstream investment managers to take social and environmental issues seriously?

DB: Informed committee members are key. It is often difficult to take on the "suits" but when you come armed with good information it's easier. Seek out other union trustees and/or committee members for help and advice.

The keepers of the workers' money are the pension trustees. It's a bit of a thankless job given the volatility of the markets and the general dissatisfaction that we all have with anyone that is looking out for our long-term interests.

Peter Chapman, the executive director of the Shareholder Association for Research and Education (SHARE) and long-time shareholder activist, believes that pension plans are turning to shareholder activism because they believe it adds long-term value to the plans' investments. In an interview in June 2003, Peter said:

The primary purpose of a pension fund is to provide financial security for the retirement of plan members and beneficiaries. But retirees also have broader interests, including the well-being of their families and communities, and those of other workers. Pension plans are powerful economic institutions to which governments have granted special tax status in order to meet the goal of a secure retirement for workers. New regulations in many OECD countries require pension funds to report on how, if at all, they take social and environmental considerations into account in the investment decision-making process. This broader interest of retirees and the responsibility of pension funds as powerful social institutions provide a solid foundation for pension trustees to ensure that they meet their financial goals in a constructive and responsible manner.

DOES IT WORK?

There's a difference of opinion in the investment community about the effectiveness of pension fund activism. Some critics claim that activist pension funds like CalPERS are not focusing on their main duty — maximizing the financial gains of their funds. Critics suggest that some activist funds are putting personal politics ahead of their financial responsibilities. I guess they've got a point — if access to clean air, water, food, and human dignity are considered personal politics.

COMMUNITY INVESTMENT: ACTING GLOBALLY AND LOCALLY

BY CORO STRANDBERG

I met Coro Strandberg in 1995 at a social investment conference in Vancouver, British Columbia. At the time, she was a director of the board of Vancouver City Savings Credit Union, known as VanCity. When I told her that I was fairly new to the investment business and intended to focus entirely on social investing, she immediately got to work introducing me to people that she thought could help. Over the years, many of us have been able to count on Coro's brilliance in bringing together like-minded individuals. She brings intelligence and passion to community-driven social change.

As GLOBALIZATION ADVANCES around the world, deep divides are created in its wake. Many point to the growing disparity between the rich and the poor, both within and between nations. Others point to the lowering of environmental standards to accommodate corporate priorities. Regardless of one's point of view of the impacts of globalization on world poverty and environmental health, the facts remain:

- One billion people live on less than a dollar a day.
- The Earth's ecosystems are degrading at an estimated three percent a year.

These figures are not going to be turned around any time soon, and certainly not without the active engagement of people around the world — not to mention governments, business, labor, and civil society.

So how can people around the world have an affect on this outcome? How can ordinary people help to reduce deprivation and hopelessness and improve environmental conditions at home and overseas?

COMMUNITY INVESTING

Community investing is a proven method for the concerned individual to help reverse these trends. It creates opportunities for investors and financial consumers — anyone reading this book — to address the deep-seated needs of local communities bypassed by the globalized economy.

What is Community Investing?

Community investing (CI) is financing that generates resources for people and projects that are not well served by the traditional banking sector or have difficulty accessing capital through conventional channels. Called cause-based, socially directed, or alternative investing by some, community investing is an opportunity for the average investor or financial consumer to allocate a portion of their investment portfolio or to invest their savings with financial intermediaries that are dedicated to improving local or third world socio-economic and environmental conditions.

Community investors seek opportunities to place their money in investment vehicles and savings accounts where their dollars create jobs and affordable housing, develop local enterprise, provide community services such as child care, improve the environment, empower workers or consumers, and reduce overall world poverty.

Community investments pay different rates of return from zero to less than market, and occasionally, even market rates. Those offering the lowest rates typically have the greatest social impact, transforming the most lives in the most profound ways, or providing the greatest benefit to the environment. Sometimes, depending on prevailing interest rates, "below market" community investments can pay more than other investments. Anyone locked into a below market five-year three percent rate on a community investment deposit three years ago would likely have seen this asset outperform their mutual funds. As for investment risk, it depends on the product — some are fully guaranteed; others are not. However, many uninsured community investments have proven to be low risk over time, with loan losses from community investments comparable to traditional bank loans.

Community Investment is an opportunity for investors to maximize the impact of their investment, doing more with their money than many would believe possible. Unlike a donation, a community investment works over and over again in the local community throughout the life of the investment. While some interest may be foregone, the principal is repaid when the investment matures and the total amount invested helps people improve their lives or benefits the environment. Take a $10,000 investment in an international community development program. Invested in micro-credit funds in the third world which provide loans of $100 to help mostly women develop their micro-enterprises, that $10,000 can result in improved economic fortunes for 100 families living in the most destitute poverty conditions imaginable. It is difficult to achieve that kind of impact without spending your capital in most social programs. It is also difficult, nigh impossible, to have that kind of impact on poverty reduction through typical investment screening approaches.

Most social investors screen their portfolios so as not to invest in tobacco companies or those that pollute the environment or otherwise cause harm, while investing in those that have good labor and community relations, for example. A community investment, on the other hand, is an *active* investment in community organizations creating positive change in their communities.

Community investment is a relative newcomer to the social investment scene, emerging only recently as an asset class worthy of study. The US has the largest market for community investment, with an estimated US$ 5.4 billion in this asset class, according to 1999 figures of the Social Investment Forum. Canada's Social Investment Organization has estimated roughly Can$ 69 million in this asset class in Canada (2003), while the UK figure comes in about £250 million. Eighty-six social investment organizations in fifteen European Union member states reported a total loan portfolio of EUR 640 million, which includes those offering loans for small enterprise and the voluntary and cooperative sectors. Micro-finance institutions in the southern hemisphere have at least US$ 7 billion in loans outstanding to over 13 million individuals.[1] All in all, this represents a fraction of the world economy, but — as all of them are small loans — a considerable investment in improving poverty and environmental conditions.

As with any emerging field of study, there are few international standards for defining a community investment, hence some of the difficulties in measuring the size and growth of this sector around the world. In fact, most definitions are silent on the environmental benefits to be achieved through community investing. They are included in the present definition because of their close correlation to community well-being and because many new community investment products incorporate environmental features.

The range of community investment vehicles and methods available to community investors is growing with increased sophistication of this sector. The US leads the way with the greatest array of investment vehicles and the greatest number of investment opportunities. Some of the most common forms of community investment are described in the "Community Investment Guide for Investment Professionals and Institutions," published in September 2000 by the Social Investment Forum.[2] I have adapted this list to include environmental investing, as follows:

- **Traditional banking products** offered by social finance banks, community development banks, and credit unions including savings accounts, term deposits, guaranteed investment certificates, certificates of deposit, etc.

- **Community development or conservation-based loan funds** which provide flexible and low-cost financing for housing, environmental, and economic development projects of community development corporations, cooperatives, and other community-based non-profit organizations, offering unsecured term loans with interest rates in the range of zero to five per cent for one to ten years.
- **Community development venture capital funds** providing equity investments in businesses that hold the promise of growing rapidly to create jobs, entrepreneurial capacity, and wealth that benefit low-income people and distressed communities and which offer preferred and common stock or subordinated debt with equity "kickers" such as warrants or royalties and which may also include venture capital funds that help environmental technologies and businesses.
- **International funds** leverage capital to support local organizations in developing countries dedicated to poverty alleviation and environmental improvement, provided through a number of international funds which channel investments into local organizations in developing countries.
- **Socially responsible mutual funds** that direct a small portion of their assets to support community development or local environmental enterprises.

Community investors today have a range of investment vehicles available to them, depending on their social and environmental goals, risk profile, and investment objectives. As much as every investor is encouraged to diversify their portfolio to hedge against risk and other exposures, every investor is encouraged to include community investments in their portfolios. Indeed the emerging standard is for every social investor to include community investments amongst their other investments — the US Social Investment Forum believes this should be at least one percent, an amount which would have a minimum impact on an investor's overall return. While this might not seem like much to the individual investor, applied to the Canadian marketplace, this would result in Can$500 million in

Canada and US$15 billion in the US being leveraged for community investment purposes.

There are a multitude of community investing vehicles around the world that could be described to convey the range of CI approaches. The following two are profiled as both are full-service banking institutions, invest their capital in community development, and offer community investment products. As such they ably demonstrate a range of approaches available to community investors. The last is profiled because, while not a full service financial institution, it is a fully licensed bank providing savings accounts and investment products in support of community investment domestically and internationally.

COMMUNITY INVESTMENT WORKS! THREE CASE STUDIES

Community Investing at Vancouver City Savings Credit Union (VanCity)

VanCity, the world's largest community-based credit union, headquartered in Vancouver, BC, Canada, is a full-service financial institution offering a wide array of banking products to its 292,000 members. With Can$8 billion in assets, it is a significant provider of home and commercial mortgages throughout the Greater Vancouver, Fraser Valley and Greater Victoria regions and a Canadian leader in social investing. In 1986, it launched Canada's first socially screened mutual fund, Ethical Growth Fund, which is now part of a family of screened mutual funds owned by the Canadian credit union system under the brand name Ethical Funds Inc.

Since the pioneering days of its socially responsible investing in the mid-eighties, VanCity has evolved its array of social investment products, with an increasing focus on community investment. Consistent with VanCity's purpose, which is to work with people and communities to help them thrive and prosper, VanCity is committed to the principles of social justice, economic self-reliance, and environmental sustainability. This ethic is manifest at the consumer level in the following products:

Deposit Programs

VanCity's Community Investment Program offers two deposit products, one local and one global. Both are eligible as a Registered Retirement Savings Plan (RRSP) and carry the same guarantee as other term deposits with the credit union.

The first community investment deposits (CID) earn a slightly lower rate of interest and benefit communities in VanCity's service area. Investments are pooled for the purposes of investing in projects that enhance the local quality of life, including environmental protection, affordable housing, and community economic development. Financial assistance is provided to projects in the form of low interest loans, reduced rates on mortgages, and other credit services. As an example, the Mental Patients' Association was able to benefit from a community investment deposit discounted mortgage to purchase Hampton Hotel, a 46-unit single room occupancy facility that provides safe, secure, and affordable housing for people with mental illness living in the Downtown Eastside, Canada's poorest neighborhood.

The second community investment deposit product, the International Community Investment Deposit (ICID), is similar to the CID in that it, too, is a below market investment. Investors are able to choose a rate of return from zero to two percent (which from time to time, depending on prevailing interest rates, could be an above market investment), and 100 percent of that investment is channeled through international community lending agencies to provide credit in low-income communities around the world. With an investment pool of Can$2 million, investors can be confident their funds are working to support families such as that of Ramadevi Shankar. Growing up in a small Indian village where family wealth is measured in cattle, Ramadevi was determined to have a cow of her own one day. Working from dawn to dusk ironing her neighbors' clothes as a way to earn the $225 she would need, after ten years she managed to save only $135. Through a loan fund supported by VanCity's ICID investors, she was able to get financing to buy her first cow — and more. Today she has a thriving dairy business.

By spring of 2003, VanCity members had deposited over Can$4 million in these two community investment deposit products.

Loan Programs

While traditional businesses are the recipients of the bulk of VanCity's business loans, VanCity has dedicated resources to support the growth of the micro-enterprise sector with the objective of reducing poverty and creating jobs for those who have a business idea but are unable to access traditional credit sources. They have also established financing and support programs for businesses who seek to improve the environment through their products, services, or internal practices.

The VanCity Peer Lending Program is the oldest of these programs, providing the first building block of small business credit to members. Peer Lending provides affordable small loans of $1,000 — $5,000 to those who may lack assets, traditional collateral, or a credit history. Often benefiting very low income people, including those on welfare, the peer group nature of the program provides support and advice from peers, networking and learning opportunities, and exposure to new customers. Access to subsequent loans (up to $5,000) is based on the repayment record of all members within a group. Group members act as the loan officers, evaluating each member's loan request. Since its inception in 1997, the VanCity Peer Lending Program has lent out over Can$1 million to 257 borrowers with 624 different loans.

VanCity also offers Self Reliance Loans to those who cannot access traditional financing, providing loans up to $35,000 to VanCity members or those who have graduated from a self-employment or entrepreneurial training program. Traditional business financing requires collateral, and many low income people do not have the business or personal assets to provide the security sought by conservative banking institutions. Self Reliance Loans provide a way for these businesses to get ahead on the basis of the applicants' character and credit history and the viability of their business. Since its inception in 1997, Self Reliance Loans have provided more than 800 entrepreneurs with over Can$11 million in financing to support job and business creation in Greater Vancouver. The Self Reliance Loan portfolio is one of the largest micro-loan funds in North America, supporting businesses such as Nana's Kitchen and Hot Sauce to start and strengthen their businesses.

Beginning as a small restaurant run by sisters Nasim and Shelina Mawani, Nana's Kitchen quickly determined that there was a greater demand for wholesale products. As the sisters were unable to qualify for conventional credit due to limited personal net worth and business track record, VanCity provided expansion financing. The company now manufactures and distributes frozen and fresh East African food such as sauces, wraps, samosas, and chapattis for large retail customers and has seen annual revenue increases of 140 percent to reach sales of over Can$700 million.

VanCity also offers ABLED loans (Advice and Business Loans for Entrepreneurs with Disabilities), which provides loans for micro-enterprise startup or expansion to people with disabilities who have experienced difficulty accessing credit and business services. Loans are based not on personal assets, collateral, or security but on an individual's business plan and strength of character. VanCity provides the services of an enterprise development specialist to provide business mentoring and support.

On the environmental side, VanCity offers a full range of Green Business Loans to help small and medium-sized businesses, cooperatives, and non-profits achieve their business and environmental goals. This includes conventional business credit through VanCity Credit Union, growth capital through VanCity Capital Corporation, and a tailored Conservation Loan Fund for eligible businesses with strong business plans but unable to access conventional credit. Through a partnership with Ecotrust Canada, an environmental capacity-building and finance organization, VanCity aims to expand the conservation economy in British Columbia by strengthening the enterprises that help to bring it to life.

One such enterprise is Canadian Eco-Lumber Cooperative whose members are eco-certified wood producers, woodlot owners, and their advocates. Working together, VanCity and Ecotrust Canada found innovative ways to use grants, Community Investment Deposits (above), and the Conservation Loan Fund to help the cooperative further develop its market for eco-certified wood.

Finally, VanCity Capital Corporation, a Can$25 million subsidiary of VanCity, provides financing to green economy businesses, cooperatives, and non-profit enterprises dedicated to improving the quality of life. One such example is the Cooperative Auto Network (CAN). An urban car-sharing service, CAN currently has 56 vehicles in its fleet serving over 1,100 members, effectively removing 230 cars from the road and reducing greenhouse gas emissions by 490 metric tons (540 short tons) a year.

Another example of VanCity Capital's role in financing green economy business, is Furry Creek Power, a BC-based independent power producer with a focus on small-scale green hydro projects. When completed, Furry Creek will produce enough electricity to power 8,000 to 10,000 homes — while offsetting the equivalent of 25,000 tons per year (22,680 metric tons) of pollutants that would otherwise be released into the air by a typical thermal gas generating plant.

VanCity and it subsidiaries are an example of a mission-based financial institution that uses some of its core assets to finance sustainable development and that brokers investments of its members to help improve local and international world conditions.

Community Investing at ShoreBank

Since its founding in 1973, ShoreBank has been increasing economic opportunities in inner-city urban and resource-based rural communities. As the first community development bank in the US, they have invested more than US$1 billion in their priority communities — those traditionally underserved by other banks — and minority owned companies. They have created, retained, or placed nearly 11,000 jobs and have rehabilitated 38,000 units of housing, while investing US$305 million in small businesses since their inception.

They started out in Chicago's South Shore, providing banking services in areas red-lined by traditional banks, and have gradually expanded their operations such that now they operate commercial banks in Ohio, Illinois, Michigan, and the Pacific Northwest. In 2002, their priority communities — designated communities where ShoreBank focuses its resources to achieve impact — included 13 neighborhoods in Chicago; Detroit's East Side; eight neighborhoods on Cleveland's East Side; Michigan's Upper Peninsula; and western Washington and Oregon.

With current overall consolidated assets of US$1.4 billion, ShoreBank also operates a real estate development company, a not-for-profit organization in each of their five priority markets, a consulting company, and a mezzanine finance company — all of which support ShoreBank's mission to build strong sustainable communities, protect and restore the environment, and help their customers build wealth.

Through its diverse operations ShoreBank also provides financial and home-buyer education, debt consolidation and credit repair service to hundreds of clients a year. To help lower income customers build their personal assets, ShoreBank runs a matched savings program, matching customers savings accounts — 181 of these individual development accounts (IDAs) were active by the end of 2002, helping people save for an education, a small business, or a home down payment. In 2002 they also provided over 200 people with entrepreneurial training, provided financing to business start-ups, and placed hundreds of people in jobs.

ShoreBank operates a full suite of banking products and services (including personal and business loans, retirement and investment services, checking and savings and cash management) and offers a number of community investment options. Over 4,000 individuals, corporations, and non-profit organizations have supported ShoreBank's work by placing deposits in ShoreBank's banking subsidiaries — US$324 million at year end 2002. These Development DepositSM and EcoDeposits® are channeled into ShoreBank's mission-based investments to support their overall community and sustainable development objectives.

Development DepositsSM

Development Deposits support ShoreBank's community development work. They offer the same features and market rates as other bank deposits and are equally federally insured. The bank converts these ordinary bank deposits into development loans.

At ShoreBank, "community development investment" is defined as loans made to individuals, non-profits, or businesses located in their priority areas; real estate loans made for properties located in priority areas; loans made to minority-owned companies located outside priority areas; new construction or rehabilitation undertaken by ShoreBank affiliates; down payment assistance grants; and conservation loans.

Development Deposits go to finance businesses such as the one owned by Lillie Kinnard in Chicago's South Side — Kinnard Realty and Management, LLC. Lillie received financing for her first project from ShoreBank in 1993, when she wanted to help provide safer, more livable, housing for low-income people in the community. Since that time ShoreBank has helped Ms. Kinnard purchase and renovate 25 apartment buildings to provide affordable housing for hundreds of families.

During 2002 ShoreBank placed US$ 207 million in underinvested communities in the US and oversaw the disbursement of another US$60.5 million in overseas development. ShoreBank designs, implements, manages, and advises loan programs in local banks and loan funds in developing and transitional economies with capital from major financial institutions. This international financing has totaled US$203.3 million over the past 13 years.

EcoDeposits®

EcoDeposits® mirror Development DepositsSM in every way, except that they offer community investors the opportunity of supporting the work of ShoreBank Pacific, the first regulated financial institution in North America dedicated to sustainability-based economic revitalization. ShoreBank Pacific works to fulfill its mission to create a conservation economy in the rainforest of the Pacific Northwest by targeting its lending to local companies that use energy efficiently, work to reduce waste and pollution and conserve natural resources. In 2002, EcoDeposits® attracted US$57 million in deposits.   ·

Tri Vitro Corporation in Kent, Washington, has benefited from the EcoDeposit® program. They received their first loan from ShoreBank Pacific to buy new processing equipment for their recycling business, which now recycles glass into sandblasting abrasives, water filtration media for swimming pools, mosaic tiles, and landscaping products. Subsequent financing, in the form of a line of credit, from ShoreBank has helped them grow into a highly profitable business while diverting waste from the local landfill.

ShoreBank Pacific lent out US$12 million in 2002, and across the group, ShoreBank financed a total of $56 million in conservation loans for hundreds of conservation projects. Through this program ShoreBank is creating new economic opportunities that also protect the environment. Borrowers have used the proceeds to conserve energy, reduce negative environmental impact, produce "green" products and market to "green" consumers, significantly extend the useful life of old buildings, and restore abandoned buildings to productive use. Their Pacific companies focus on organic farming, environmentally responsible fishing, producing non-timber forest products, redeveloping contaminated sites, and financing green buildings.

ShoreBank, like VanCity, is another community investment model, leveraging savings accounts and term deposits from across the US to support their mission to build communities, enhance environmental conditions, and help their customers build wealth.

Social Banking at Triodos

Triodos Bank, based in the Netherlands with additional branches in Belgium, the UK, and, in 2004, Spain, is Europe's leading social finance institution, offering a range of targeted and regular savings accounts and investments. Their purpose is to achieve social, environmental, and cultural objectives in day-to-day banking. While not a full service financial institution, they nonetheless offer a number of savings and investment products which channel investments to enterprises which add social, environmental, and cultural value in fields such as renewable energy, social housing, complementary health care, organic food and farming, and social businesses. They also finance Fair Trade and micro-credit organizations in developing countries.

Founded in 1980, Triodos Bank was launched in the Netherlands with EUR 540,000 share capital issued to a number of investors, today totaling 7,000 private individuals, banks, insurance companies, and pension funds — all of whom are interested in supporting the development of responsible businesses working for social renewal. These investments typically provide a market rate of return and, while not listed on stock exchanges, are traded privately through Triodos Bank.

Over the past quarter century, Triodos Bank has initiated a number of funds and today is an active manager of funds set up by both the bank itself and for third parties, including charities, donor organizations, and governments. Some of their funds include Triodos Venture Capital Fund, Solar Investment Fund, Triodos Green Fund, and the UK and Dutch Wind Funds. The Triodos Venture Capital Fund is a private equity fund that invests in companies in the expansion phase. Target companies in this fund include organic food, renewable energy, energy efficiency, and environmental products and services. Solar finance includes business development, support and investment capital to companies that provide solar photo-voltaic and other energy sources in developing countries.

The Triodos Fair Share and North-South Funds support both small and micro-businesses in developing countries which have no access to financial services or local commercial banks, and Fair Trade that provides local farm producers a living wage. Recently, the Triodos Fair Share Fund issued more than 50,000 shares, raising over EUR 1.5 million.

Some of the businesses financed by Triodos in 2002 include:

- Deshaboina, a farmer in India received a loan from Triodos-sponsored Indian Basix Bank, to buy a milk buffalo. He now sells milk at the local market and was thus able to save to invest in his rice fields.
- Organic food shop, Rio de Bio, in Utrecht, deals exclusively in whole foods, selling more than 3,000 organic products in their shop.
- Skelian Clinics, a group of seven chiropractic clinics spread over the Cotswolds in southwest England, specialize in the diagnosis and treatment of joint, muscle, and bone problems.
- Buro Kloeg in the Netherlands produces communication materials about nature, the environment, eco-tourism, and horticulture. Buro Kloeg works primarily for local authorities and environmental organizations, producing information panels, folders, books, games, and reading packages.

By year end 2002, over EUR 729 million was invested in the savings accounts of over 65,000 Triodos Bank depositors. Triodos provided nearly EUR 400 million in financing to over 2,700 enterprises, showing the power of this model to mobilize capital and invest in sustainable development and social innovation. In all, Triodos Group manages EUR 1.3 billion in assets, with an expansion plan to bring their unique model of social finance to other European countries and beyond. This impact and scale likely exceeded the expectations of the initial small group of visionaries meeting in the late sixties studying ways for money to be managed consciously.

Triodos, like VanCity and ShoreBank, provides another approach to social banking, in which community investors can use their savings and their investments to wield a greater good.

THE SCOPE OF COMMUNITY INVESTING

As these case studies demonstrate, there are a range of options available, for those interested in using their resources to make a difference at the community level. Not only are there social finance and community development banks providing savings and investment options, as described here, but there are mutual funds — such as Real Assets and Meritas in Canada — which dedicate a portion of their investments to community development investments, and there are foundations and other organizations, such as the Calvert Foundation in the US, which provide tailored investment opportunities to investors concerned about improving socio-economic conditions domestically and internationally.

Community investing, however, remains an emerging asset class and not yet as popular — or as available — as screened and active shareholder funds. Indeed, only a modest number of credit unions are committed to community investment in Canada. In the US, a larger number of credit unions, under the banner of the National Federation of Community Development Credit Unions, are active in this way. The UK credit union system is still in its nascent stages of development. There are an increasing number of loan funds offering retail investments and a number of community development bank programs operate in the US. There is a network of social finance banks in Europe — International Association of Investors for the Social Economy (INAISE) — which offers mission-based investment opportunities. Community development venture capital is another emergent industry very much in its infancy.

So a challenge confronts community development investors and community development intermediaries who face significant barriers to their collaboration. Both those working to improve local conditions through finance strategies and those wanting to improve local conditions through their personal investments need to find each other to make their community development visions a reality.

INVESTING IN COMMUNITIES AT HOME AND AROUND THE WORLD

As these case studies have attempted to show, community investing provides one opportunity for anyone with investments or simply a savings account to help improve conditions locally or internationally. Community investment yields multiple returns: it earns a modest rate of interest and is later returned to the investor or saver, while yielding real social, economic and environmental benefits to individuals and communities — such as jobs created, houses built, lives transformed, and environment restored.

Is it difficult to confront, let alone grasp, the realities of world poverty and environmental deterioration? It can be overwhelming for those of us busy with families, earning a living, and making our own ends meet. However, mission-based investment and savings programs are available to most of us, bringing home the potential to create opportunity and hope in the lives of the most disadvantaged and to restore precious environmental eco-systems. While it is true that the globalization of our economy has created winners and losers, it is also true that there are opportunities within our reach to make a difference where it really counts. We can chose to bank with financial institutions working to make this difference and to invest in community investment products that are channeled to poverty-reducing and environmentally oriented initiatives. We can follow the principle of allocating one percent of our investments to community development. And we can know that our wealth is working overtime to contribute to the wellbeing of people and eco-systems around the world.

Community Impact: Dave Mowat

Deb Abbey talked to VanCity CEO Dave Mowat, about leveraging its resources to create positive change in the communities where it operates.

Deb Abbey: How do you differentiate VanCity beyond being a member organization?

Dave Mowat: In our statement of values and commitments we talk about being a leader: this is a defining feature for VanCity. We've got eight billion dollars in assets and we've got a whole machine set up to write loans and take deposits. So when we want to launch a new cutting-edge product like our international community investment deposit, we simply deploy that machinery and that can lead us in some interesting directions. If someone without that infrastructure wanted to create an international peer lending deposit to raise funds they would be faced with a whole set of overheads. We already have the machinery in place and we find innovative ways to use it. So whether it's our international community investment deposit, our peer lending program, lending to people to help them get off social assistance or lending circles — they're all opportunities to use the basic infrastructure and skills that we have in the organization and try and apply that in the broader community. We use our core competencies to create positive social change in the world.

DA: Are there leaders that you admire?

DM: There are a lot of great companies. I think that there are even more great leaders inside companies that are moving them in the right direction. I personally believe that the best companies in the world are moving toward greater social responsibility. They understand that they live and breathe their brand and the confidence that consumers have in them. So when a great company sees people boycotting its products, it learns from that rather than treating it as an annoyance. It's about thinking about where the company will be twenty years from now — and that means thinking about the environment and social issues. Because great companies understand that they are a part of society.

DA: When a company puts itself in a leadership role like VanCity, there's bound to be some flak. Have there been issues where you've had to do some damage control to preserve your integrity as a company?

DM: When there's controversy, we have to take a stand on things that we believe in. But sometimes things aren't as black or white as you'd expect. In our region the issue of management of natural resources is important to British Columbians, so of course it's important to VanCity. We've had controversy around logging old growth timber. We always have to balance community and the environment. So instead of being on one side or the other, we try to encourage a dialogue between stakeholders. We ask our members to vote on issues. We have an Enviro-Visa card that contributes a portion of the value of the cardholders purchases each year to environmental causes. Our members determine what those will be.

DA: How do you keep improving, where do you go from here?

DM: I think that you just have to make sure that you don't think you know it all. While we might be successful, there's always something new to learn. As one of the most influential financial institutions in British Columbia, we've got the ability to promote best practices and to integrate them into the organization. And that's absolutely critical if we don't want them to remain marginalized. It isn't enough to theorize and discuss these things in academic circles. We help get them in to the mainstream so that everyone can look and learn.

DA: Are there other financial institutions that you would consider role models?

DM: There are a number of credit unions in Canada that try and make a difference. Assiniboine Credit Union in Manitoba and Metro Credit Union in Toronto have done some great things. I think the international banks like Triodos and the Co-operative Bank in the UK are great role models. The big banks in Canada are trying hard, but when you're big, philanthropy is the easiest thing. We're more connected to the community, and so we try to be involved in community issues.

DA: How do you build corporate social responsibility into the organization? Really hard-wire it so that everyone lives and breathes it.

DM: I think it needs to make sense and it needs to be balanced. Whether it's a consumer buying a product, a person deciding to join VanCity, or VanCity employees selling a green loan product or a green deposit product or an international community investment product — it needs to be well-managed and it needs to make sense. People need to see the benefit to themselves and to the community. It's easy to give money away, but when you're finished giving it away, it's gone. The ability to actually recycle your impact on the community is huge and that's what we really look for. We want to create sustainable solutions that continue to have a significant impact on the community.

DA: Tell me about some of the social programs you've started in the company.

DM: Well, VanCity Capital would be a key one — VanCity Capital was something that I came here to help VanCity create. It uses VanCity's financial capability to create a fund of money for rapidly growing companies, trying to provide financing that borders on equity. And it really tries to create growth in the local economy by providing risk capital to really well managed businesses. So we've got something that virtually no one else offers. The ten million dollars that VanCity Capital has put out there has created several hundred jobs locally: that's significant in our community. VanCity Capital also earmarks a portion of the capital to lend to non-profits and cooperatives — and there we're completely at the cutting edge and feeling our own way. As governments provide less and less services for people, non-profit organizations are performing more and more of those essential services. We see organizations with 20–30 million dollar budgets — these are significant businesses. In the past, non-profits haven't built assets — they haven't created value in their organizations the way that a company would. A company uses equity and a company uses debt. Henry Ford would never have sold a car if he hadn't invented the car loan. The corporate world is really familiar with borrowing: for a new building, a new computer system, to lease premises or equipment, or simply to hire new people. Companies raise money on the capital markets by issuing stock or they borrow money. Non-profits have never had that luxury, so they tend to operate budget to budget. And in this day and age government doesn't have a lot of budget capacity, particularly for overhead. So we looked for a way to use the business model of providing leverage in a non-profit setting. It's potentially a very big win if we can make it work. It gives the non-profit sector a whole set of tools it didn't have before.

If you are interested in pursuing community investment opportunities, see the Resources section at the end of this book.

BETTER BUSINESS, BETTER WORLD: LEADERS WHO ARE CHANGING BUSINESS FROM THE INSIDE OUT

BY ADINE MEES

I met Adine Mees when I joined the board of Canadian Business for Social Responsibility. Adine was then a departing board member and cofounder of the organization; as its current president, she's come full circle. Adine loves to share her successes and challenges and she's certainly learned a few things on her journey. I came to know her through mutual friends and was thrilled to be invited to become "Ask An Expert" on the Citizens Bank website when she was vice-president of marketing and corporate responsibility. We are fortunate to have Adine as a leading advocate for corporate social responsibility in Canada. She has lots of practical advice for employees who want to effect positive change in their own workplace.

ADVANCING THE SUSTAINABILITY agenda within business has to be one of the most challenging careers. Most business professionals have a solid grasp of what good financial performance looks like but very few of us understand how to track, manage, and report on a company's social and environmental impacts, let alone merge the three into an integrated bottom line. There is no Executive MBA in Corporate Social Responsibility (CSR). In fact, there are few academic programs aimed at CSR leaders at all. Couple that with the fact that the field is still emerging and complex and that its mandate stretches across an entire organization, and it's a wonder that anyone would take it on. The people profiled in this chapter have not only adopted a CSR agenda, they have embraced it as internal advocates making enormous efforts to advance the field.

Some common character traits emerged. All of the people interviewed approach both their work and their life with courage, initiative, innovation, optimism, and integrity. They wouldn't be successful if they didn't. It's hard to get up every day and face critics both inside and outside your company when your mission is comprehensive, complex, ill-defined, and you don't have a clear road map. The reality is that staff inside the company will range from supportive to neutral to negative.

Critics within a company tend to be concerned about the speed of change and the impact that it will have on their lives and careers. Critics outside the company tend to be concerned that the company isn't changing fast enough. Developing a balanced approach and finding common ground with both groups becomes increasingly important. Finding a core group of supporters is equally, if not more important. These people, both inside and out, remind you how far you've come: they hold your successes up for you to recognize and celebrate.

Regardless of the challenges, none of those interviewed, myself included, would trade what we do for any other experience. We love what we do. We deliberately sought out employers and business ventures with a strong values alignment. We want to make the world a better place, and we believe that business can be a powerful engine for that change.

STARTING OUT WITH A CSR LEADER

I want to start you out with a few words of wisdom from Bob Elton, BC Hydro's executive vice-president of finance and chief financial officer. Bob has 27 years of corporate experience behind him, giving him a good sense of perspective. When I asked Bob what kind of legacy he'd like to leave at BC Hydro, he described a vision of decreased energy consumption and of meeting future demand growth with clean energy. He cautioned me with patience. "While it's necessary for us to set ambitious and clear targets, the reality is that it takes ten years to build anything well." This is a good reminder that a longer-term view is essential: it doesn't matter if you are in year one, three, or five — we are all working towards improvement and we will get there with each other's encouragement and support.

He also cautions that as a CSR leader, it's important to "be good at all the bottom lines." Taking responsibility for social, environmental, *and* financial bottom lines will help you get key stakeholders on board early on and could save you from some push back down the road.

Pearls of Wisdom
Talk it up. This is a recurring theme of Bob Elton's. The harder it is to have the conversation, the more reason to do it. Talking in small groups or one-on-one is easier than with larger groups. Go out on a limb — typically people respond well.

The Random Acts of Goodness Strategy

I wish I'd talked to Bob Elton before I began my ten-year CSR career with the VanCity group of companies. Given that my CSR career developed within VanCity during the time that CSR emerged and later advanced, my story in this chapter begins with a great deal less sophistication than it ends.

It all started when I applied for a new job posting. I can't remember the exact job title, but it was something along the lines of community affairs coordinator. The position had bumped around from one side of the corporate head office to the other, finally finding a home in human resources. It was essentially a blank canvas with a mandate from the board and CEO that a strong community engagement strategy be developed. Since the former community affairs coordinator had spent a great deal of time and effort funding sports programs, I felt it necessary to declare in the interview that I wasn't particularly interested in attending soccer or football games. Thankfully, neither was my soon-to-be-boss.

The next five years were a whirlwind of activity. With strong direction and support from the board of directors and resources allocated by the executive, the scope and responsibility of that position grew with each year. When I started, we had an annual philanthropy budget of $80,000. When I left five years later, we had a CSR team of seven staff directing a plethora of CSR programs and initiatives and, much to the chagrin of the CFO, a philanthropy budget of over $1 million dollars. I like to call this, my first approach to CSR, "The Random Acts of Goodness Strategy."

The Random Acts of Goodness Strategy was for the most part void of strategy and full of good intentions, innovation, and energy. The driver was a moral imperative rather than a business imperative and so while we celebrated our many "firsts" as recipients of numerous awards and media write-ups, our accountability in the first few years was minimal. On one hand this was positive because it fostered a creative risk-taking environment. On the other hand, we weren't addressing the objections of those people who might not see the same value in this program that we did. Eventually, we would transform our CSR agenda into an integral, accountable element of VanCity's business strategy.

Early Lessons

My next adventure was at a VanCity start-up subsidiary — Citizens Bank of Canada. I had been recruited from the parent company by the CEO who wanted me to bring a CSR agenda, in line with the parent company's commitment and reputation, into this national on-line e-bank. I'll never forget my first day at work there: it was one of those experiences that has provided me with many valuable lessons. I arrived for my first day with little fanfare and was ushered into a small cubicle in the back corner of the company's information technology group. I had no staff, no budget, and though I was not yet part of the executive group, I reported directly to the CEO who had created the position.

As I sat down to survey my new work space and business cards, I realized that I had absolutely no idea what I was going to do, and for that matter, what my new job title meant. Where did the commas go? Was I the Manager of Social Policy Planning and Development or was I the manager of Social Policy, Planning and Development? One little comma could have a big impact. The first lesson? It didn't matter where the commas went. If I didn't know what my title meant and what I was supposed to be doing, neither did any of the staff, executive, or board of directors. Needless to say, it took a while for us to get some momentum going on the CSR front.

My second rather painful lesson happened shortly thereafter. One of the bank's longer-term senior executives invited me to lunch. He began the conversation by complimenting me on the work I had done at VanCity before joining Citizens Bank. He then politely informed me that as a low-cost service provider, there simply weren't the resources to advance a CSR agenda at Citizens Bank. He hoped I would understand. My second lesson? It didn't matter that the CEO had courted and recruited me and that she entrusted her child to my care when she traveled out of town. If key staff and board members in the company didn't see the value or the opportunity, this wasn't going to go very far.

So things didn't start off smoothly, but thanks to several trusted advisors and mentors, my last few years at the bank were incredible. In those last three years we revisited the bank's vision, mission, and position statements. Together the executive team drafted language that incorporated a responsibility agenda and listed key performance competencies that we needed to be able to deliver on. We already had a solid list of more traditionally accepted core competencies such as risk and reputation management, but to this list we added items such as social and environmental issues management and stakeholder engagement. We then merged the marketing and CSR functions to ensure that CSR was embedded into the company's products and communications. This was followed by the launch of an overarching ethical policy that governed the bank's investments, operations, and supplier relationships — a Canadian banking first.

When I compare my two experiences, the first at VanCity that developed organically and the second at Citizens Bank that was more policy-driven, I can see the merits in both approaches. Ultimately, what the participants in this chapter will tell you is that you need to work on many fronts with many business tools all at the same time. While the Random Acts of Goodness Strategy may have worked for many of the early CSR adopters, it is quite likely that it won't work as well in business now. As more companies in the mainstream are adopting a CSR agenda, developing a clear plan for action and a corresponding business case is becoming the norm rather than the exception. Many best practice case studies have been developed and you can save time by learning lessons from others who learned the hard way. Good places to go for support are Canadian Business for Social Responsibility (<www.cbsr.ca>), Business for Social Responsibility in the US (<www.bsr.org>), and Business in the Community in the UK (<www.bitc.org.uk>). Benchmarking best practices in your sector is a good first step and one that will save you time and money in the long term.

Once you've completed a benchmarking study, you will want to define the scope of your work. Until you've done this for yourself and your colleagues, you will get sidetracked by too many ideas and opportunities. Unless you've set a stake in the ground and defined the impact for your company in terms of opportunity and risk, all ideas and suggestions will sound interesting and you will feel like you need to look at them all — an overwhelming and often impossible task for someone just starting out.

One of the first things I did when I joined Canadian Business for Social Responsibility (CBSR) was to document my experience to create a road map for others to use. This road-map approach, titled *Building a Corporate Social Responsibility Plan: Using a Systems Approach,*[1] can be accessed on-line through CBSR's website (<www.cbsr.ca/resources>). It's a systems approach to building a CSR plan and, ultimately, a culture.

Each of the following people is well-read and well-versed in business management systems and tools. However, it's important to realize that their CSR knowledge is, for the most part, knowledge gained by doing. Peer learning is one of the most effective forms of professional development — thus their stories and experiences will provide valuable insight and learning for others in the CSR Field. If you are currently a CSR professional or interested in entering the field, consider these profiles as a passing of the torch of sorts — a chapter of peer mentors. Not that any of these people are considering retirement: they simply want to pass along some of their more valuable lessons learned.

MAKING A BETTER CONTRIBUTION: IAN WARNER, PRESIDENT AND CEO, CITIZENS BANK OF CANADA

Founded in 1997, Citizens Bank provides financial services through the Internet and its 24x7 call center. Citizens Bank is the only bank in Canada with an eight-point ethical policy on key social and environmental issues. President and CEO Ian Warner describes his early career days as a foreign exchange trader in profit-driven terms. He entered the workforce in the 1980s when, as he says, "The mantras were 'greed is good' and 'you're only as good as your last month's profit and loss contribution.'" He spent time as a trader in Japan and then returned to Canada, eventually rising to the position of vice-president of treasury and credit for Citizens Trust Company. Ian found himself a good fit — his trading values at that time were consistent with the solely profit-driven values of Citizens Trust. But when VanCity credit union acquired the company and brought in a new CEO, Citizens Bank of Canada was born — and a whole new world began to unfold outside of Ian's office.

Ian chuckles as he remembers his first attempts to work with the change. "The CEO began introducing a CSR mandate and I was carried pretty much kicking and screaming all the way in the beginning." If you haven't already guessed, this is the same senior executive who sat me down and gave me a reality check in my first days at Citizens Bank. That's why it's my turn to grin when he responds to my question about what his greatest challenge is today. "Once you get it, you think that everyone else is going to get it. And they don't. Not always." Ian spends his time these days listening to the guidance and advice of key people who he refers to as his CSR mentors — primarily those staff entrusted with embedding the bank's CSR strategy and programs.

As we finish up, Ian leaves me with a final thought. "Everyone here has the capacity to make an impact, to become a quiet everyday hero." Through his progression from cynic to skeptic to advocate, Ian has become one of my favorite quiet everyday heroes.

A BALANCED APPROACH: RON NIELSEN, DIRECTOR, SUSTAINABILITY AND STRATEGIC PARTNERSHIPS, ALCAN

Pearls of Wisdom
Focus your resources to have a greater impact. Your company has an infrastructure in place to make money. Understand how this can be best leveraged for greater social impacts.

Originally a subsidiary of Aluminum Company of America (Alcoa), Alcan Inc. became an independent Canadian corporation in 1928 and is now a $13-billion organization and the parent company of an international group operating in many aspects of the aluminum and packaging industries. Alcan's customer pledge is "Imagination Materialized" and the company has an expansive network of operations in 38 countries with 52,000 dedicated employees and a global customer base.

Unlike Ian Warner, Ron Nielsen's CSR career was a natural evolution and extension of his previous work history. Prior to making the leap over to the corporate sector as Alcan's director of sustainability and strategic partnerships, Ron worked in several government and non-governmental agencies, developing a strong background in environmental management issues. Ron has put his natural sense of optimism and inherent drive to succeed to good use while working for Alcan.

Ron is unique amongst his peers in his ability to bring to his work a practical understanding of the three sectors that are needed to foster action on sustainability: government, NGO, and corporate. The breadth of his experience has given him a natural ability to understand the barriers and constraints that other sectors face when it's necessary to find common ground and common solutions. Although Ron describes himself as passionate about making a positive contribution, he exhibits one of the most balanced approaches to CSR that I've seen yet. And since his work at Alcan is focused for the most part on organizational change with a company of 53,000 employees, a balanced approach seems to make a lot of sense. Wisely, he cautions against the CSR leader who might inadvertently be bringing personal perspectives, values, and baggage into the organization and culture.

> ***Pearls of Wisdom***
> *The two most important characteristics a company needs to possess in order to advance a sustainability agenda successfully are the capacity to lead and manage organizational change and the ability to innovate.*

Ron spends much of his time as a translator, interpreting the complex concept of sustainability and "turning it around into the language of the various corporate departments and divisions." He suggests that there is little value in talking to the finance department in the language of triple bottom lines at the outset. Rather, he suggests that we invest time in understanding the primary responsibilities of the key players in our companies and think about how sustainability applies to them.

A DIFFERENT KIND OF CORPORATE ADVOCACY: LAURA DE JONGE, MANAGER OF SOCIAL RESPONSIBILITY, NEXEN

Nexen Inc. is an independent global energy and chemicals company formed in 1972 that has 2,000 employees and annual revenues of $2.6 billion. Nexen states that it operates under a system of 'total governance,' which means board, management and employees work together to meet corporate goals and foster a culture of integrity throughout the company.

Laura de Jonge, Manager of Social Responsibility for Nexen, is one of the most enthusiastic CSR leaders that I know. Like Ron Nielsen, she is full of optimism and drive and, like many of her other counterparts, Laura comes to the field of CSR indirectly, holding positions in a variety of seemingly unrelated roles before landing in her current job four years ago. The diversity of her experience both inside and outside Nexen gives her the ability to understand and prioritize CSR from many different perspectives.

Her story is an interesting one. When she was feeling that she'd given and gotten the most out of her last position, she approached management for a reassignment. Instead of waiting for someone to make her future happen for her, she decided to try to help it along. Laura put time and effort into a unique proposal to management — to assign her to be the first Nexen employee to participate in the Calgary United Way Loaned Rep program, a three-month volunteer assignment to work with other corporate volunteers. Following this experience, she met and debriefed senior management at Nexen, including the CEO. She concluded her presentation with a line she grins about now, "When you're supporting a campaign like this," she said openly, "you're creating more love in this world." She tells me now that she can't believe that she used the "L" word in the boardroom, but that it was important to her at the time to touch them at a profoundly human level, the way that she'd been touched through the experience.

Laura got a call the next day from the senior vice-president, general counsel. His gift to her? A book by Jean Vanier called Becoming Human. Laura followed this up with another proposal to management, this time including her recent community development experience. The result was an offer to develop a new job as Nexen's first manager of corporate responsibility.

Like many of us who get started in this field, Laura didn't yet have a full sense of what she was getting into. She says that if she'd known what she was starting when she first took on the corporate responsibility advocacy and implementation roles within Nexen, she might have been too terrified to do it. Much like Ron at Alcan, Laura managed through those first few years with loads of optimism and a drive to succeed.

Given the chance, she would do it all over again, but next time she'd spend more time enlisting the company's human resources and investor relations professionals — people she now has identified as key to the success of her work. Her experience within Nexen, a company she chose to work for because of its strong reputation and values, is that people will rise to the expectation that they do the right thing at work, just as they would at home. Her goal is to inspire people towards the corporate responsibility agenda, not to impose it on them. "The talk is the easy part. It's the walk that's really hard."

REDEFINING VALUE: GORDON LAMBERT, VICE-PRESIDENT OF SUSTAINABLE DEVELOPMENT, SUNCOR ENERGY INC.

Suncor Energy Inc. is a publicly-traded Canadian energy company that employs 3,400 employees and in 2003 expects to produce 250,000 barrels of oil equivalent a day. Suncor's vision is focused on three priorities: increasing shareholder value, reducing its environmental footprint, and contributing to the well-being of the communities in which it operates.

Much like Laura de Jonge at Nexen, Gordon Lambert, Suncor's VP of sustainable development, works on the sustainability agenda within the Canadian energy sector. His interest in integrating the three pillars of sustainability — economic, social, and environmental performance and impacts — dates back to his days in university. This was in the late 1970s, before much progress had been made on the business and sustainability agenda. With an early calling to this field, Gordon combined course work in biological sciences and economics.

Pearls of Wisdom
"CSR is intuitively the right thing to do but not all people are intuitive. That's why I need to develop the messages in a way that makes sense to the staff." Lesson learned from Laura — have patience.

"I had a genuine intuitive sense that there was a strong connection between business and the environment during these early years," Gordon recalls, "and later the Brundtland Commission validated this for me." The Brundtland Commission was the 1983 UN World Commission on Environment and Development that coined the term "sustainable development" which it defined as meeting "the needs of the present without compromising the ability of future generations to meet their own needs."

Much like his peers, Gordon Lambert didn't have his sights set on the job he has now when he first started out. After graduating from the University of Guelph, Gordon signed up to manage an environmental impact assessment for a heavy oil project in Cold Lake, Alberta. He sees those first four years in the field as a critical learning opportunity.

"Those four years provided me with an equivalent of ten years experience," he recalls. "What I learned up there, you don't get taught in school. As the face of the company in the community, I learned quickly how important it is to take into account the interests of stakeholders." Although the transition from academic life to tackling issues front and center for a community was an intense experience for him, he remembers it as being a very positive one; "We were tackling issues that were very real for the people in this community."

Like his peers, Gordon was attracted to Suncor because of its reputation. When he joined, the CEO and senior management team had recently embedded sustainability into the company's core purpose statement. While his earlier work may have come more out of a compliance mind-set, his title, position, and influence within the company now speak to a powerful message that the sustainability agenda is not peripheral. Rather, it is central to the success of Suncor as it strives to expand its business whilst navigating and adapting to constant change.

Suncor hasn't always benefited from the strong positive reputation it enjoys today. I asked Gordon to talk about how they turned the company around. His first strategy was to focus on the top 40 people in the company — people with power and influence.

"I needed to convince them to be open to looking at sustainability concepts in a more thorough way," he remembers. "We gave ourselves two years for this phase and seeded conversations as often as we could. Many of these took place at our management retreats and were led by sustainability thought leaders like Amory Lovins from the Rocky Mountain Institute. We asked ourselves questions like: What does it mean to be a sustainable energy company?"

This approach seems to have paid off for Gordon and for Suncor. These days Gordon describes himself as running to keep up with the many innovations coming from within the company. "I find myself identifying and supporting other change agents across the company," he says. Now he tries hard to stay on top of all that is going on around him — from aboriginal business development to solar car washes and wind farms. Gordon's response to those people who want to debate whether Suncor should be doing all this? "We're too busy doing it to get engaged in the debate."

A New Definition of Leadership: Tazeem Nathoo, executive coach and former senior vice-president of operations, Vancouver City Savings Credit Union (VanCity)

According to Tazeem Nathoo, "If you've got the support of the leadership in your company — you can climb mountains." As a corporate change agent, Tazeem has scaled a few mountains in her time. While in senior management at BC Hydro, prior to her career at VanCity, Tazeem led programs that focused on employment equity and the advancement of women in trades, technology, and leadership. She was attracted to her first position at VanCity, vice-president of human resources and environment, because of VanCity's leadership in these arenas.

Tazeem was impressed early on with VanCity's track record which included the review of declined loan applications submitted by women; peer-lending programs; a culture of work and family balance; the intentional advancement of women into senior management positions; environmental leadership; and excellent community engagement strategies. However, Tazeem remembers that, while it was easy to understand the CSR agenda at an intuitive level, in those early days she found it hard to articulate in a way that made sense to those that were unfamiliar with CSR. She credits the board of directors and her colleagues in senior management for making great strides in terms of embedding CSR into the structure of the credit union and she credits the CSR staff — the content experts — with advancing the CSR agenda at an operational level.

During her first eight years at VanCity, the CSR team reported to her while she led the human resources group and later moved into the role of vice-president of operations. "The cultural tie-in was critical," she remembers. "We had to work with staff to move the organization and its field units from doing good based on phi-lanthropy and volunteerism, to doing good based on values and cor-porate social responsibility."

Tazeem oversaw the beginning of an ambitious undertaking — the development of a set of corporate values and commitments for the credit union. She credits Business for Social Responsibility (BSR), a US-based organization of which she was a director at the time, for pointing them towards strategy leaders, and the book *From Good to Great: Why Some Companies Make the Leap ... and Others Don't,*[2] by James C. Collins, which became the basis for this work.

In its early years, the CSR agenda at VanCity was driven for the most part by the passion of the board of directors and the com-mitment and innovation of the CSR staff. Later, she credits the company's social audit process and it's statement of values and commitments as being strong drivers — across all functional units and through all levels of staff.

"For staff, in their day-to-day corporate life, finding meaning in their work can be a powerful driver," said Tazeem as we began to finish up. "That is where the magic comes from." Tazeem credits the development of many of VanCity's progressive innovations (e.g., the Community Investment Deposit, the Ethics in Action Awards program, its award-winning social audit and its peer lending pro-grams) as coming from that place of passion and magic.

When I began my conversation with Tazeem, I asked her where her courage and commitment comes from. It can be challenging and exhausting to work on a change agenda. She smiled when she told me that growing up as a Muslim woman, she developed an ethos of balance at a very early age — doing well and doing good went hand in hand. She doesn't see it as a trade-off or being about compromise. Tazeem also tells me that she feels that the Canadian values of jus-tice, equality and humanity resonate strongly with her values as well as the values inherent in CSR. "And," she says, "if you work on advancing these issues, you get used to working with resistance."

She concludes our conversation by telling me something that all CSR leaders feel from time to time: "When you are passionate about the work you are engaged in, it feels so good and compelling that you give your soul." She then tells me something I've experienced as well. When you are a change agent, there comes a time when you get tired. Tazeem is now re-energizing herself and her work by coaching other leaders to develop their lives with vision and purpose.

AN ENGINE FOR CHANGE: DAVID DEMERS, FOUNDER, PRESIDENT, AND CEO OF WESTPORT INNOVATIONS

Incorporated in 1985, Westport Innovations Inc. is dedicated to leading the shift in the international commercial engine industry from oil-based to gaseous fuels and is the leading developer of gaseous fuel engine technologies. Total revenue for the last fiscal period was $24.6 million and the company currently employs 200 people. Technology development alliances are in place with a number of leading engine manufacturers, including Cummins Inc., MAN, Isuzu, and BMW.

Pearls of Wisdom
Hold people accountable. Integrate CSR into performance management and performance objectives.

I first met founder, president and CEO of Westport, David Demers, when he opened a Canadian Businesses for Social Responsibility (CBSR) conference — The Green Venture Forum — as the keynote speaker. Since then he has become a great supporter of CBSR and, from time to time, a mentor of sorts to me. I will never forget his first words when he described the business opportunity he saw in green energy for Westport.

"I don't do this because I'm an environmentalist," he said. "I do this because it makes great business sense." While he may have taken this line because of his audience — a group of traditional and social venture capitalists — I have since learned that David sees corporate social responsibility as a win-win-win: for business, the environment, and society.

As an entrepreneur and business leader, David sees the concepts and values of CSR as consistent with his personal values and the values of the company's emerging markets. David grew up in Saskatchewan, the birthplace of Canada's medicare system. These kinds of programs, he says, "came out of a strong sense of community and the need for community to band together to survive."

I am interested in David's story because he is a classic entrepreneur in every sense. His company is mission-based. He is an optimist and risk-taker. He is driven, and in turn, he is a driver of change. While many of today's CEOs — those at large publicly traded companies — may be engaged for an average of two years in any given job, David is there for the long haul. "Corporate boards of large companies typically hire someone to come in and fix a problem," says David. "The focus then is on short-term outcomes which often results in short-term thinking."

While David thinks that this trend may shift back, he clarifies that: "As the founder of an early-stage public company, I work to balance a longer-term vision with having to prove the company's value each twelve months. My leadership comes from combining vision with reality and a close connection to the market." He is quick to add, "Course-correcting is a big part of what an entrepreneur needs to do if they are going to successfully move a new or mature venture into the future."

Pearls of Wisdom
Understand that entrepreneurship is a process of discovery. Though you may not have a crystal clear vision early on, success will lie in your ability to understand and respond to emerging changes and opportunities.

These are lessons that apply to both entrepreneurs and intrapreneurs — those that develop and implement new ideas and concepts within larger companies and organizations. One final lesson from David: always maintain a sense of humor and grace regardless of where your share price is. When I think of my conversations with David over the past year and a half, this is how I see him — in a constant state of good humor and grace, even when under fire.

FROM CORPORATE ACTIVIST TO CONSERVATION ACTIVIST: LINDA COADY, VICE PRESIDENT PACIFIC REGION, WORLD WILDLIFE FUND CANADA AND FORMER VICE-PRESIDENT OF ENVIRONMENTAL ENTERPRISE, WEYERHAEUSER CANADA

Weyerhaeuser Company is an international forest products company with annual sales of $18.5 billion. The company was founded in

1900 and currently employs approximately 58,000 people in 18 countries. They have ranked in the Fortune 200 since 1956 and number one in the forestry industry in Fortune Magazine's annual corporate reputation survey for seven years.

Linda Coady's story is interesting from the perspective of change management. For more than ten years she worked as a change agent within a company that underwent massive and sometimes turbulent internal and external change. She was in the process of leading change on the sustainability agenda within MacMillan Bloedel, a Canadian forestry giant, when Weyerhaeuser acquired it. For Linda, approaching the CSR leader role with a background in public and government affairs gave her an ability to translate and communicate key sustainability issues both inside and outside the company, a skill that would become increasingly important to her own and the company's success.

Linda began her career in CSR with MacMillan Bloedel, where she served as their director of government affairs. She worked on environment and land use issues, often from a crisis management perspective. "I remember," laughs Linda, "that there was this big MacMillan Bloedel protest that happened just at the time that the entire senior management group was out of town. The protesters were out in front of our corporate head office with a big blow-up chainsaw that was four stories high and blocking traffic in all directions. They came in and chained themselves to the empty desks and chairs on the executive floor and suddenly the building was surrounded by police and helicopters."

Linda and her colleagues in the public affairs group found themselves in charge of a situation that was getting more tense and chaotic by the minute. How did they handle it? They ordered in lunch and served up sandwiches to everyone.

"It was funny and made everyone — the protesters, the employees, and the police — relax a bit," she remembers. "That night, the national media coverage showed people eating and talking together." Although this didn't go over as well with the entire executive group when they returned, it was shortly thereafter that the company president called her up and offered her the job of vice-president of environmental affairs.

With no job description to guide her, Linda set up office next to the president and got to work. With a new role which had developed out of controversy and crisis, her mandate was simply, "Fix it." With that, she points to the obvious: "When you are appointed in a crisis, you don't ask what to do. You start bailing." During the first four years, her work was primarily focused on solving external problems. "The company was losing money: environmentalists had targeted us in Canada and internationally and we were in the process of losing our CEO."

One of Linda's first steps was to set up a group of advisors, both inside and outside the company. This involved cultivating strong supporters within the company and building relationships with important stakeholders, such as environmentalists and First Nations groups, outside of the company.

Linda knows that those first conversations happened, for the most part, because many of these people saw her as their access point to the company's decision makers — something they may not have had previously. While Linda may have started her new career at a time when protests were the communication tool of choice, she was eventually able to engage some of her fiercest opponents to work on a solutions agenda with her.

"In the beginning, a lot of people came from the starting point that the company shouldn't be in business," remembers Linda. "It started out with some very heated conversations but then eventually switched to a mode of looking for solutions." Together, Linda and her informal external advisors developed a capacity for joint problem solving that was based on listening, understanding, and trust. According to Linda, "Issues became the point of connection and then the relationships developed."

While the first phase of Linda's work was externally focused on issues management, the second phase became internally focused on change management. A new CEO was appointed whom Linda describes as being "prepared to make changes on the ground. He wanted us to develop a strategy that would move the wood off the mountain and into the mill in a way that was safe, profitable and sustainable," remembers Linda. The new CEO, Tom Stephens, set the vision and then followed up with formal change mechanisms: resources, accountability, timelines, and reporting relationships. Ultimately, the greatest change happened when Weyerhaeuser acquired MacMillan Bloedel. Prior to, during, and after the acquisition, Linda became the internal conservation champion and pioneered exciting new best practices within the Canadian forestry sector.

She remembers with fondness two special projects that exemplify this time of creative change and innovation at MacMillan Bloedel and later Weyerhaeuser: the Vancouver Island Marmot Recovery Program and Iisaak Forest Resources, a joint venture in eco-forestry between Weyerhaeuser and the five Nuu-Chah-Nulth First Nations in Clayoquot Sound. As the company's internal conservation champion, she made sure that at every internal conversation and meeting she was a part of, she raised the issues of conservation and sustainability.

"We eventually changed the DNA of the company as well as the sector," she points out. By internalizing the conservation debate, Linda strengthened the company's ability to respond to and overcome concerns of key stakeholders.

As a mover and a shaker, and someone not unfamiliar with controversy, Linda is finding solutions that fully integrate social, economic, and ecological needs. Delivering on this front requires determination, intelligence, courage, and a heavy dose of optimism. Whether she realizes it or not, Linda Coady — through her innovative approach to business and the environment — exemplifies a new and welcomed generation of leadership.

> **Pearls of Wisdom**
> *Embed CSR into the culture of the company. Lead change within the company by engaging problem solvers and working with a team across the full spectrum of the company. A word of caution: If you don't, your work may become marginalized and you may inadvertently become the corporate lightening rod when issues arise.*

A UK Perspective: Mallen Baker, development director, Business in the Community

Business in the Community (BITC) is a business-led network of more than 700 socially responsible companies in the UK As the largest national UK organization of its kind, their member companies employ over 15.7 million people in over 200 countries worldwide. In the UK, their members employ more than one fifth of the private sector workforce.

I liked Mallen Baker, BITC's development director, the minute I met him. David Wheeler, a mutual friend who heads up the Business and Sustainability Program at the Schulich School of Business, introduced us in Toronto. Mallen had crossed the Atlantic to talk to a group of Canadian business leaders about accountability and reporting. He had just launched an ambitious reporting project for Business in the Community (<www.iosreporting.org>), and was in Canada to talk about its impact. Mallen likes to look at the complexities and ambiguities of CSR and explore them, not only as ideas but also as part of the search for practical solutions. He has a website that is definitely worth a visit (<www.mallenbaker.net>), and if you have time for more reading, an e-newsletter for the CSR leader that is topical, relevant, and most importantly, short.

Mallen started his career by working with small and medium-sized businesses, helping them to understand their environmental impacts and improve their environmental performance. "I learned to sell on business benefits and use the process of change as the sales tool for future steps. If I'd gone in preaching sustainability on day one, I would have never gotten in the door," he wisely says. Balancing the speed of change is a challenge for business.

"Taking companies from the point of where they have been told that it was all about their community programs to the point where they need to be prepared to consider all the aspects of how they create value as a business — that change is a challenge for some. Others have really shone, however, and it is a constant joy to work with some of the creative, committed companies out there," says Mallen.

We both agree that working with a company to position them as a leader in the face of complex issues is tough because it does require a certain pace of, and commitment to, change. Mallen Baker describes today's leaders as those people "who have a powerful rapport with their audience, because of their empathy and a communication style that is direct and no-nonsense. They have relentless determination to build solutions when others around them can only criticize."

A SUMMARY OF LESSONS LEARNED

Although each of the CSR leaders profiled in this chapter approached their mandates with different skill sets and backgrounds, they share some valuable lessons learned. These lessons will be useful to you regardless of where you are positioned within your organization or whether your organization is a small or medium-size company or a large multinational enterprise.

Pearls of Wisdom
Learn to say, "No."
Don't try too many things or take on too much too quickly. When the program is in its early phases and you are still finding your way, there will be many people with ideas and inspiration and it is hard to turn down an opportunity to make a difference.

Lesson One: CSR is really about change management. Many of us engaged in this work are tasked with embedding new values into the company. As CSR advances, more companies with traditional missions are seeing value in layering on CSR concepts. To succeed, all of our leaders agree, you need to hardwire CSR into the company's DNA — through a formal change management process.

Lesson Two: Revise your corporate structure and appoint a dedicated CSR leader. This person needs to have the support of the CEO, to work cross-functionally across the full spectrum of the company, and to understand how (s)he is adding business value.

Lesson Three: Engage people and build relationships. All of our leaders consult with formal and informal advisors — inside and outside the company. Don't seek out only people who agree with you; find those who question your company's actions and work with them to understand the issues and the opportunities.

Lesson Four: Although you'll be pioneering some out-of-the-box thinking within your company in your effort to minimize the company's negative social and environmental impacts and to maximize the good ones, you need to work with the business strategy and planning people to ensure CSR becomes a part of the company's overall vision and mission.

Lesson Five: Develop a support network at work and at home. This work is exhausting and complex and requires you to work across the entire organization and at all levels of management. Be good to yourself and find ways to energize yourself. A sustainable future depends, in part, on your success.

Before you begin working with this list, remember Bob Elton's advice at the beginning of this chapter: It takes time to build something well. Temper your optimism with patience and enjoy the journey for what it is — the change that you can make and the learning you will acquire along the way.

For more resources to help you find your way through the quandaries of CSR, see the Resources section at the end of this book.

GETTING STARTED ON STRATEGIC GIVING FOR SOCIAL CHANGE

BY TIM DRAIMIN AND DRUMMOND PIKE WITH AMY STEIN

After many years in the international development community, Tim Draimin brought his considerable expertise to Tides Canada, a foundation dedicated to social investing through philanthropy. Since Tim joined Tides Canada just as I was launching Real Assets three years ago, we've done a lot of commiserating about the rewards and challenges of launching our respective enterprises in the worst bear market since the 1930s. Nevertheless, both of us have weathered the storm and our organizations are strong and vital; I expect they'll be around for the next bear market and the one after that. If you want to promote social and environmental well-being through your donations, Tim Draimin can help you craft a successful strategy.

Drummond Pike is the founder and president of the Tides Foundation, and he is also president of the Tides Center, Groundspring.org, and Highwater Inc. Drummond was a founder and associate director of the Youth Project following a long student involvement in the anti-war movement of the late 1960s. He also served as executive director of the Shalan Foundation from 1976 to 1981 and helped to found Working Assets in 1983.

I N A WORLD GRIPPED by so many social and environmental challenges where many remedies have been found wanting, one of the most important developments has been the rise of civic organizations committed to promoting new ways to create positive social change. This chapter describes how social investors can craft a strategy to ensure maximum results from their gifts to charitable, grassroots, and community organizations.

Who do you give money to? How much? Why? For many people, the answer is that we give money to those who ask, if we feel we have any to spare and if we're sympathetic to the cause. Most people give reactively, not strategically. There are so many worthwhile causes that prioritizing our donations is a challenge. And there are so many urgent causes that directing donations toward long-term social change and root causes of problems requires determination. Getting strategic about giving for social change takes more effort than responding to the knock on the door or the plea in the mail, but it's more effective — and more rewarding.

Social change giving directs money to organizations working to solve root causes of social justice or environmental problems, as well as to mitigate their symptoms. Strategic giving is a planned, deliberative approach to maximizing the impact of donations. These two tactics are highly complementary, together offering you a powerful way to direct your money or time to the environmental and social justice issues that are most important to you.

Just as financial investors seek financial returns, donors who are social investors expect a social return from their investment in society. Social investors typically take a more business-like approach than traditional charitable donors: they are more engaged, more inclined to link their contribution to the anticipated outcome, and they perform more due diligence. In the words of the Social Enterprise Alliance (<www.se-alliance.org>), a social investor "considers gifts of time, property, or money not as mere charity, but an investment in sustainable social change."

Before explaining how to become a more strategic giver, this chapter discusses why the funding of social change efforts is critical, describes the current funding environment, and reviews several trends.

WHAT'S IN A NAME?

A note about terminology: Organizations that exist to serve the public benefit, and which are distinct from profit-seeking business or government, are variously called non-profit, NGO (nongovernmental organizations), voluntary sector, independent sector, third sector, or civil sector. Civil sector usually refers to the broadest cross-section of organizations, including universities, hospitals, and religious institutions, as well as social service agencies and social change activists. Some are also registered charities, providing tax receipts for donations they receive, but Canadian and US tax laws differ in their definitions of registered charities.

Figure 10.1: Numbers of registered charities and other non-profit organizations
Credit: Amy Stein. Source: Giving USA 2002[1]

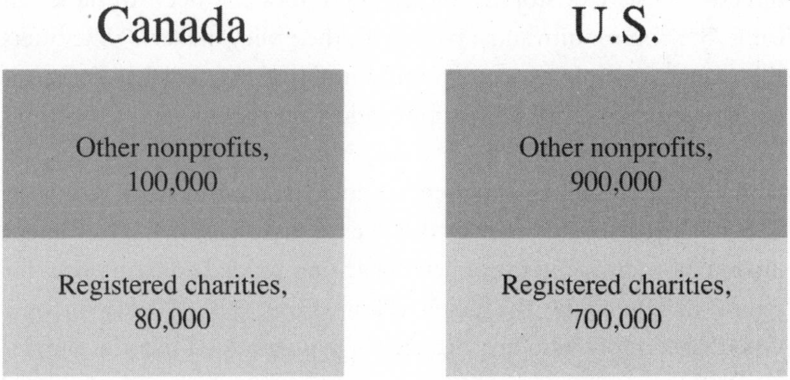

Canada	U.S.
Other nonprofits, 100,000	Other nonprofits, 900,000
Registered charities, 80,000	Registered charities, 700,000

For more information, refer to the Internal Revenue Service (<www.irs.gov/charities/charitable/>), and the Canadian Customs and Revenue Agency (<www.ccra-adrc.gc.ca/tax/charities/>).

VITAL SECTOR UNDER STRESS

Non-profit organizations tackle many issues that would otherwise be ignored. They are an early warning system, identifying urgent social issues, such as growing economic disparity, discrimination, and the decline of urban communities. They pinpoint environmental problems, such as toxic drinking water, unsustainable forestry practices, climate change, and endangered habitats. Non-profits often form in response to an acute local issue. Many of them, as they identify root causes, start making linkages through which they mature into long-lived groups with a global perspective: "acting local and thinking global." Charitable giving enables them to do this.

Non-profits can also play a critical role as incubators for social innovation. They are community-based, researching and testing alternative solutions to complex societal problems. They develop answers and turn them into templates that government or the private sector can adopt and scale up.

St. Christopher House in Toronto is an example of an organization that has taken on a dual mandate of providing direct services while pursuing community development. Susan Pigott, executive director of St. Christopher House, describes the need to have "an ear in the community and a voice with the policy makers." She offers the recent example of a community undertaking social policy project, through which St. Christopher addresses significant income policy issues for low-income people. A targeted grant allowed St. Christopher to hire an experienced policy analyst to work with staff and volunteers. The analyst discovered that current government income programs and tax policies have unintended consequences for seniors living below the poverty line. Over 300,000 low-income Canadian seniors who are eligible for a guaranteed income supplement were not receiving it.

St. Christopher addressed this issue on two fronts. It continued its direct service to the seniors, including tax clinics informing them of their rights, while gathering data and developing a community involvement strategy with a team of staff, income policy experts, and volunteers. It has been a challenging process, but eligible seniors are now automatically informed by Ottawa that they can apply for the low-income supplement.

In addition to creating benefits through specific endeavors, the civil sector as a whole plays an important role in society.

Government, business, and the civil sector form a balance that determines how effectively a society functions. As experts like Peter Drucker explain, a strong civil sector is fundamental to accountability and effectiveness of businesses and democratic governments. For example, we can see around the world that where civil society is weak, authoritarian governments can flourish.

Where would society be without agencies devoted to caring for the poor, the housebound, the homeless, and the hungry? Far from stepping in to fill the gap, governments and corporations often show less commitment to helping in areas where there is little advocacy or attention. Consider also, for example, how PEN helps protect freedom of the press, Greenpeace spotlights environmentally irresponsible practices and proposes solutions, Democracy Watch scrutinizes government actions, and the Anti-Defamation League defends the rights of minority populations. Where would society be without these and countless other organizations like them, engaging corporations and governments in an ongoing campaign for greater accountability and fair treatment?

These questions are not just rhetorical. The non-profit sector is under tremendous stress from increasingly restrictive funding, reduced donation levels (adjusted for inflation), and downloading of services from governments to non-profits. A 2003 Canadian study conducted by Katherine Scott for The Canadian Council for Social Development warns that the viability of the non-profit sector appears to be at risk under the prevailing funding regime. In her summary report, Katherine explains the difficulties:

> Many organizations that survived government funding cutbacks of the 1990s are financially fragile because they are now dependent on a complex web of unpredictable, short-term, targeted project funding that may unravel at any time.... Much organizational time is now devoted to chasing short-term sources of funding, often at the expense of the organizations' mission and core activities.[2]

And while major donor funding has become more problematic, individual charitable giving has dropped off. The stock market downturn, the terrorist attacks on September 11, 2001, and the war in Iraq and SARS in 2003 have combined to heighten anxiety about our continued prosperity. Many people have become more conservative in assessing their wealth, and more hesitant about giving away any portion of it, despite the urgent need for such gifts.

THE CHALLENGES OF SOCIAL CHANGE PHILANTHROPY

It can be especially difficult as a donor to form a commitment to finding long-term solutions. We in the developed world have become disconnected from the impacts of our actions. If we buy clothes made in a foreign sweatshop, or throw hazardous household waste into the garbage can, there is no immediate or direct consequence to us. We may not even know there is anything wrong. It is hard to imagine how our individual actions can have any impact, whether good or bad, on environmental and social justice issues which sometimes seem bigger and more complex every year (or week). We want to do the right thing, but trying to take a stand against so many long-term, widespread problems can feel overwhelming.

The key to moving beyond immobilization is to start aligning our actions with our values, and to find other people who share these values. Although most of us don't have the time, the energy, or the inclination to become full-time activists, giving for social change directly connects our desires for a better world with organizations and activists who share our passions and are working together to bring about positive change.

For Tracy Gary and Melissa Kohner, authors of the book, *Inspired Philanthropy: Your Step-by-Step Guide to Creating a Giving Plan,* social change philanthropy — which "analyzes and responds more to cause than effect" — is fundamental:

> Most giving falls into the traditional or charity model of responding to acute, immediate crisis needs — blankets and food for flood victims, temporary housing for homeless families... Traditional philanthropy is also

very good at supporting the established institutions — educational, research, religious, social and cultural — that maintain and improve mainstream society and its structures....

Social change philanthropy seeks to identify and address the root causes of disadvantage or practices that threaten values such as equity or a healthy planet ... For homeless people, a sweat-equity program of home building and private-public partnerships for job training and education might provide more permanent solutions to their needs than shelters and food kitchens.[3]

Greater donor awareness is needed to help agencies tackle root problems. Even when organizations are funded for the direct service portion of their mandate, it is rare to find donors willing to assist them in tackling systemic social justice issues. Donors like to see the direct impact of their money — but often, the strategies that social change groups must employ to address root causes of societal problems are painstaking, indirect, and hard to measure in the short term. Activities include, for example, advocacy, coalition building, demonstrating, grassroots organizing, and public interest law.

The story of *Blue Vinyl* offers an example of how a global environmental health problem is being combated by funders and activists working together. Vinyl, also known as PVC or polyvinyl chloride, is widely used in siding, flooring, window frames, toys, medical equipment, cloth and paper coating, packaging, and countless other plastic products. Charitable dollars funded the production of *Blue Vinyl* (<www.bluevinyl.org>), an award-winning 2002

Many people see the wisdom in the aphorism, "Give a man a fish and he can eat for a day. Teach a man to fish and he can eat for a lifetime." Social change groups take this a step further. Recognizing that problems like hunger have myriad causes, these groups support hungry people to ask tough questions: "Why doesn't society teach all people how to fish? Who owns the pond? Who wrote the rules about how ponds get used, and how can they be changed?" Social-change philanthropy supports people to work for fundamental change in political, economic, and cultural institutions.
— Anne Slepian and Christopher Mogil, *Welcome to Philanthropy*[4]

documentary by Judith Helfand and Daniel Gold that humorously conveys a serious message about the severe toxicity of vinyl during every stage of its life cycle. Environmental groups around the world had already been campaigning against vinyl, but the documentary catapulted the issue into the public awareness. The filmmakers have leveraged the popularity of *Blue Vinyl* by linking up with many environmental groups and together launching "My House is Your House" (<www.myhouseisyourhouse.org>), a community education and consumer organizing campaign against the vinyl industry. The campaign's 27-page toolkit for consumers includes a vinyl fact sheet, a policy introduction page, sample resolutions against PVC and dioxins, and dozens of names of individuals and organizations involved in the global fight to replace vinyl with cost-effective, safer alternatives.

VENTURE PHILANTHROPY

Since the late 1990s, venture philanthropy has emerged as a challenge to the more common project funding approach described above. Many major new donors are business entrepreneurs, who see themselves as investors in social change rather than as traditional donors. Having succeeded in business, they want to apply their skills in identifying and shaping excellent early-stage non-profit ventures as well. They offer management expertise and strategic assistance to leverage their financial investment, which is not limited to grants but may also include loans and other financial instruments.

Non-profit Enterprise and Self-sustainability Team (NESsT), an international non-profit promoting venture funding, describes venture philanthropy as:

> ... an emerging field of "engaged philanthropy" that combines the policies and practices of long-term investment and venture capital models with the principles and public benefit missions of the non-profit sector. VP strategies combine financial capital "investments" with some form of additional capacity-building or technical assistance to the non-profits they support. Some of the key distinguishing characteristics that define the VP

approach include: multi-year financing, tailored financing, "engaged" relationship between investor and investee, organizational focus, shared risk, agreed benchmarks for success, and exit strategy.

— NICOLE ETCHART AND LEE DAVIS[5]

Is venture philanthropy really new? Alan Broadbent, a board director of Tides Canada, has a long history working in the areas of social justice and non-profit funding as chair of the Maytree Foundation. He points out that at each wealth-creating boom since the Industrial Revolution, new people entered into the philanthropic arena with a clear sense of purpose and strategic design — from Andrew Carnegie through to Ford and Rockefeller, and more recently Turner, Soros, Gates, and Skoll. (See Broadbent's speech on this topic at <www.tidescanada.org>.)

An increasing number of foundations have started applying a venture capital framework, prompted by a desire to maximize the impact of their grants on the long-term effectiveness, accountability, and sustainability of non-profits. One expanding VP phenomenon is Social Venture Partners (<www.svpi.org>). Founded by technology sector philanthropist Paul Brainerd, Social Venture Partners is a venture philanthropy giving circle model now spreading to over 20 North American cities.

Forward-looking foundations and grant-makers are grappling with how to better understand and apply social return on investment, using tools for measuring outcomes and impact, for evaluating potential grantees, and for use by charities. In some ways the new venture philanthropists are more demanding than other donors, establishing measurable benchmarks (such as target numbers of individuals served each year), conducting frequent assessments, and requiring a plan that enables them to exit the organization eventually. But in other ways venture philanthropists are far less restrictive: they recognize that to truly leverage their money they have to invest in organizational capacity. They recognize that too many non-profits struggle to maintain quality programs without appropriate investments in infrastructure, technology, and staff training.

MORE QUESTIONS THAN ANSWERS

Can venture philanthropy presume too much? Does a business approach adequately address the complexity of social change issues? How should social return on investment be measured in a group working to improve the sustainability of agricultural practices, or to save the whales? How will an infusion of business sensibilities mesh with charitable values and a mission-driven, activist culture? Why is it presumed that executive directors would benefit from advice and close monitoring from their funders? That there are more questions than answers at present is to be expected, considering that venture philanthropy is intended to provide long-term funding and benefits, and the vast majority of initiatives are less than five years old.

SOCIAL ENTREPRENEURSHIP

The rise of the venture philanthropists has accelerated a wave of new social enterprises and highlighted the value of social entrepreneurship in strengthening non-profits. Social enterprises generate earned income to support their mission-based activities. Academic J. Gregory Dees defines social entrepreneurs as those who:

> ... play the role of change agents in the social sector by adopting a mission to create social value (not just private value), relentlessly pursuing new opportunities to serve that mission, engaging in a process of continuous innovation, adaptation, and learning, acting boldly without being limited by resources currently in hand, and exhibiting a heightened sense of accountability to the constituencies served and for the outcomes created.[6]

A primary attraction of the social enterprise model is the potential for self-sustainability, reducing the organization's dependence on an array of short-term restrictive program grants and resource-intensive fundraising. The capacity of business-oriented venture philanthropists to help social enterprises develop the skills to run a successful business is one of the great strengths they can bring to the relationship.

Venture philanthropy funding of social enterprises is not just for foundations or technology sector millionaires. Social investor forums connect enterprising non-profits with audiences of prospective mid- to high-level donors. After a rigorous selection process, approximately six to ten social enterprises are coached in business planning and presentation skills, preparing for an evening in which they present their plans and funding needs to a roomful of potential donors. The donors are individuals who are able (but not compelled) to make a minimum donation varying from $250 to $2,500, and the money is considered an investment, albeit not one with direct financial returns to the investor.

Tides Canada pioneered Canada's first Social Investor Forum in partnership with the United Way of Greater Toronto. Other forums have been held with great success in Boston, San Francisco, and Seattle. Not only do social enterprises learn valuable business skills through the coaching process, they often secure significant funding, in-kind assistance, office space, or board members.

INVESTING IN SELF-SUFFICIENCY

After receiving a large investment windfall, Bill Young founded Social Capital Partners (<www.socialcapitalpartners.ca>) in 2001 to provide venture philanthropy funding for Canadian non-profits. As Social Capital Partners investigated investment opportunities, Bill discovered that restrictive funding conditions designed to improve accountability without investing in organizational capacity are in fact a significant and widespread barrier to the non-profit sector, forcing organizations to act in seemingly counterproductive ways in order to maintain funding sources. Social Capital Partners has revised its approach to focus on social enterprises that hire employees from disadvantaged populations, and it exclusively funds social enterprises that have a strong business model to become financially self-sufficient within three to five years. It is an ambitious target, and Social Capital Partners has found only a few enterprises that fit its criteria. But as Bill Young explains, "We believe if you don't make the financial mission as important as the social mission, you jeopardize both."

MISSION-BASED INVESTING

Just as individuals adopt a social investing approach to look at the social and environmental impacts of their investments, so too can trustees of foundations and endowments adopt *mission-based investing* (MBI) to ensure endowed resources dovetail with their goals. Mission-based investing incorporates the mission of an institution — whether a family foundation, church, school, health institution, pension fund, or scholarship fund — into its investment decision-making process.

All investments have social and environmental consequences. Using the mission-based investment process, institutions assess these consequences, alongside rigorous financial analysis, identifying risks and opportunities. For example, a health foundation may want to divest itself of tobacco stocks. A foundation committed to poverty eradication might invest in a competitive return loan to a housing cooperative (expanding social housing), rather than corporate bonds. Opportunities always exist to seek collateral benefits from investment choices by linking the investments to your mission.

Mission-based investment helps ensure that all of an institution's resources are employed in pursuit of its mission, without jeopardizing financial returns. An excellent MBI primer — including practical advice on how an institution can begin the governance process to adopt it — is *Investing in Change: Mission-Based Investing for Foundations, Endowments and NGOs,* by Michael Jantzi (downloadable from <www.ccic.ca>).

THE MECHANICS OF STRATEGIC GIVING

Given the current dynamics in the non-profit world, a strategic approach to giving is hugely valuable. When you wonder where to direct your donation to provide the greatest benefit, or how to get to the root of social problems, and when you deliberately fund certain types of non-profit work over others, you are already on the path to strategic giving. One element of strategic giving involves planning your gifts ahead of time based on your priorities, not on the fly when you get a knock on the door by someone asking for money (although you may wish to allocate a small amount in your giving plan for such requests). The other main element is considering where to direct your donation to maximize its long-term impact, and to stretch its value by looking for leverage opportunities. Two examples of leveraging are finding (or creating) matching gift challenges, and finding (or creating) giving circles.

Many giving circles are informal groups of friends, pooling their donations and getting together to select a recipient. The details vary widely. In some groups, everyone contributes the amount they would spend on dinner for two at a restaurant. The Arizona Social Change Fund meets on the fifth Sunday of any month with five Sundays.

The David and Lucile Packard Foundation in Silicon Valley focuses on protecting marine ecosystems. A priority issue for them is reversing the intensifying negative impact of farmed salmon practices on wild salmon stocks along North America's Pacific coast. With Tides Canada philanthropic counsel, the Packard Foundation has developed a strategy to fund the Coastal Alliance for Aquaculture Reform (CAAR) (<www.farmedanddangerous.org>). This support enables experienced organizations working through CAAR to undertake a coordinated range of activities — from scientific research to consumer education — to help move the salmon farming industry to sustainable practices.

Here are the basics of how to give strategically for social change, focusing on the root causes of issues you care about:

If you're feeling stuck, act anyway. Act on a small manageable piece of what you want to do. Or do something outrageous to break out of your rut. Invite friends over, and together figure out how to make gifts to organizations totaling five hundred, five thousand, fifty thousand or five hundred thousand dollars. Then make them! Shake up your patterns of stagnation, and get yourself and your money moving.
— Chuck Collins and Pam Rogers, *Robin Hood Was Right* [7]

- Review past giving and identify the causes or issues you are most passionate about: is your giving aligned with your values, or is there a disconnect? Decide what percentage of your total budget you will direct to each of the priority causes you identify.

- Determine the total amount of money you are able to give for social change at present, considering also a variety of creative ways to give.
- Do some research to identify organizations working on long-term solutions in the areas you wish to support. Make thoughtful, strategic donations to them.
- Review and renew your strategy, maintaining contact with the organizations to which you have contributed.

The rest of the chapter will expand on these steps. Although the focus here is on donating money, it is equally valuable to strategically align your volunteering time with your values.

WHAT'S IMPORTANT? WHAT'S YOUR PASSION? WHAT'S YOUR MISSION?

You might be surprised to discover how small a percentage of charitable giving goes to the areas of long-term social change. Figure 10.2 provides data from different sources on giving in the US and Canada. (The data are not perfect, as social change giving can fall into several categories — for example, religious donations also fund KAIROS, a Canadian religious coalition promoting global human rights, justice, and peace.)

What does your own giving "pie chart" look like? What do you want it to look like? How much of it will you direct toward long-term social change? Everyone's weighting of the various components of their giving plan is different. The main thing is to consciously consider the relative weighting you want to give to each area, so that your giving reflects your interests and values.

There are many worthy causes, but what social or environmental issues are you most passionate about? Giving from a general sense of altruism or obligation is less likely to be satisfying or sustained than donations targeted to an area that is especially meaningful for you. Where do you feel your money might have the most impact? Are there areas of interest you feel are overlooked?

Figure 10.2: Giving in US and Canada

Sources: Giving USA 2001; 2000 National Survey on Giving, Volunteering, and Participating; Ketchum Canada estimates[8]

Distribution of non-governmental funds to non-profits (US)

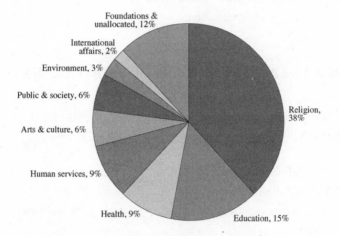

Foundations & unallocated, 12%
International affairs, 2%
Environment, 3%
Public & society, 6%
Arts & culture, 6%
Human services, 9%
Health, 9%
Education, 15%
Religion, 38%

Distribution of individual donations by sector (Canada)

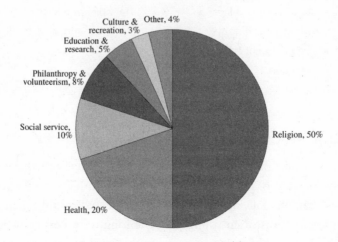

Culture & recreation, 3%
Other, 4%
Education & research, 5%
Philanthropy & volunteerism, 8%
Social service, 10%
Health, 20%
Religion, 50%

The sidebar below can help you start thinking about your focus and about how you would like to apportion your giving. Try to resist spreading your money — and your energy — thinly around many different causes. Some philanthropic counselors recommend that if you are able to give $1,000 or more, to try making gifts of not less than $1,000 each. Many people find that focusing their time and energy on one to three main causes, and perhaps one or two secondary causes, is most effective.

HOW TO NARROW THE FOCUS OF YOUR PHILANTHROPY

One area of interest to many is social justice. Which of the following subdivisions of that issue inspire your enthusiastic support?

- child labor
- children-at-risk
- community economic development
- corporate responsibility
- discrimination (age, disability, gender, race, religion, sexual orientation)
- education and literacy
- reproductive rights
- employment training, job creation

- free press
- gun control
- immigrant and refugee rights
- international development
- minority rights
- poverty and homelessness
- domestic violence
- prison reform
- war and arms trade

How Much Will You Give?

Ways of planning your donations budget vary from the simple — "five percent of my take-home pay each month" — to the torturous (for example, tallying up your assets, expected earnings, and returns on investments, then subtracting the long-term cost of maintaining your preferred lifestyle to determine the amount available for giving).

For many people, your donations budget comes out of your annual salary or investment returns, not from your savings. Allocating a percentage of after-tax income to donations is an effective method of planning your budget. A good starting point is to review how much you donated during the last few years. Could you give more? How about setting a higher target this year? When you give in monthly or quarterly increments, instead of in a lump sum at the end of the tax year, you are more likely to meet your giving target without feeling a financial pinch.

If you possess considerable wealth, your finances are probably more complex. It is beneficial to understand your financial needs and take charge of your money. Some people find management of their wealth to be an uncomfortable and emotionally laden exercise, particularly when the wealth is inherited and when other family members are involved. There are numerous resources available to assist you, such as counselors, books (such as those by Barbara Bluin <www.inheritance-project.com>), and even conferences. Tides Foundation or Tides Canada can also help you get started.

It is common for people, especially these days, to estimate their wealth conservatively — and to underestimate the amount they can give away while maintaining their standard of living. According to the 2000 data from the National Survey on Giving, Volunteering, and Participating (NSGVP), fewer than 30 percent of tax filers in Canada declared any charitable contribution whatsoever. The median level of contribution was $190. Strikingly, although wealthy people donate more in absolute dollar terms, they tend to give less as a percentage of their income than people earning under $40,000.

Challenge yourself to take a fresh look at how much you can give and consider creative ways of giving that may expand your capacity. If your income is limited, do you have any assets you don't need which could become charitable gifts? Or can you designate assets to a charity in your will?

The range of gift options is broad. Besides cash and appreciated securities, it can include real estate, art, ecologically sensitive land, and the proceeds of life insurance. Endowments can be established to continue supporting charitable purposes in perpetuity. Charitable gift annuities and charitable remainder trusts provide the donor with both tax benefits and income, and upon the donor's death the residue goes to a charity. Green Legacies (<www.stewardshipcentre.bc.ca/green_legacies_web>) outlines numerous gifting options, including more details on charitable gift annuities and charitable remainder trusts.

The biggest opportunity in charitable giving lies with the money parents will prepare to leave to their children: an estimated $41 trillion intergenerational transfer of family/estate wealth is anticipated in North America over the next 50 years. (See Paul Schervish's research on charitable giving trends <www.bc.edu/research/swri/>.) There are significant ways to protect an estate's assets for heirs and leave generous gifts to charities. Since tax rules are changing, it is important to seek legal, philanthropic, and tax advice about planned giving.

TO WHOM DO YOU MAIL THE CHECK?

Deciding upon the recipients for your donations should become much easier once you have narrowed down the candidates to those within the areas of your passion for social change. Usually, if an issue has sparked your interest, you are also aware of one or more groups working on this issue. There is no need to conduct an exhaustive search to unearth other groups working in these areas, unless you want to do so. Going beyond the organizations you're already familiar with, particularly if you have a considerable budget for giving, can help you identify new and exciting opportunities for social investment, but it takes committed time and effort.

If long-term change is important to you, make sure the organizations you've chosen have solid strategies to affect long-term change in the area they focus on. To find more information about an organization, look for its website or contact the organization for newsletters, reports, or other literature. You can look at its financial statements, but don't feel you have to understand the financial details, unless that is your area of expertise. It's important to learn about its background, its constituency, its mission, its strategy, its leader or leaders.

Non-profits are not necessarily registered charities, so if tax considerations are important to you, make sure you know which organizations can provide you with a tax receipt, and which can't.

Fear of making a mistake, or of not knowing enough to make a decision, is a common barrier to giving. Skepticism about the effective use of a donation is a related barrier. According to a 1999 survey, about 40 percent of donors said they did not donate more money because they thought the money would not be used efficiently. About the same percentage thought that charities spend too much on administration and fundraising. However, the nature of non-profit work in general, and particularly social change effort, means that success is not easily evaluated by quantitative metrics (although venture philanthropists, as mentioned above, are working to make evaluation methods more precise).

WHAT KIND OF DONATIONS HELP THE MOST?

In the May 2003 e-news of Tides Canada (<www.tidescanada.org>), board members Susan Pigott and Alan Broadbent offer these "Tips for the Philanthropically Inclined":

- Define what success looks like before the grant is made. Deciding what type of impact you would like to see will influence what strategies you choose to support.
- Don't neglect a charity's core organizational needs by funding only their program work. Many funders prefer to fund only the incremental costs of new programs, thinking they have embraced both "innovation" and "leverage" by doing so, but under-capitalization is a big reason for non-profit failure.
- Think long-term when you give. Although driven by an increased focus on accountability and results, short-term funding can sometimes put counterproductive stress on organizations.
- Make sure your giving will increase a charity's capacity for creativity and flexibility, not establish overly rigid guidelines that restrict innovation. Organizations with healthy cores can deliver their mission more effectively.

You need a certain amount of trust whenever you hand your money over to another person or group. Focusing your donations on relatively few organizations will help you give each of them more of your attention, so you can follow their efforts and observe the results. A mission you support and evidence of capable and committed leadership are more important than, for example, the percentage of funds spent on administration. Different organizations legitimately have different financial needs for their limited funds — there is no single correct amount to spend on administration. If possible, try to attend at least one event or meeting sponsored by a group you're researching, or volunteer some of your time to get a feel for the people and how the organization is run.

A common barrier to giving is procrastination — never quite getting around to writing that check. Perhaps you never finished reading the annual report, or you keep meaning to attend an event of a particular organization that interests you. Maybe you don't have the mailing address at your fingertips, and an envelope and stamp, at the same time you happen to think about that donation you've been meaning to make. And there's no deadline. The organization carries on, with or without your contribution.

Recognizing that you are procrastinating — and considering why — may be enough to help you get unstuck. If that awareness is not enough to help you move forward, then review your goals, talk to friends about them, read more inspirational materials, and set specific targets and deadlines for yourself.

No one is looking over your shoulder to hold you accountable for following through on your intentions to donate. As Chuck Collins and Pam Rogers, the authors of Robin Hood Was Right,[9] point out, "Years can go by, and no one will ask you what choices you've made about your money. It's up to you to move." They suggest that "the single biggest mistake givers can make is to think they have to move ahead completely on their own." If you are feeling stuck because you are isolated, there is a wealth of resources available to assist you. For instance, part of the mission of public foundations such as Tides and Tides Canada is to assist their donor partners in developing and implementing giving plans for social change.

WHAT NEXT?

First of all, congratulate yourself once you have sent out your first strategically targeted donations that will fund promising work in areas you are passionate about. The hardest part for most people — getting started — is over. Now your task is to keep track of the efforts, accomplishments, and direction of the organizations you have funded. Make sure you are on their mailing list; read their annual report. Also take note of other groups and initiatives that catch your attention. Perhaps create a file folder in which to collect all the non-profit news and communications that flows in. Next year, it will be time to sit down, review and refine your giving plan, and think ahead to your philanthropic goals for the coming year.

An annual planning process is frequent enough for most people, but you don't have to wait for a year to go by. Revisit your plan sooner if your money or time available for giving increases significantly, enabling you to broaden or deepen your commitments, or if you want to make major changes to your giving plan.

Your review process is a time for reflecting on your vision and your accomplishments thus far and for investigating new directions and ideas you may have to further increase the effectiveness of your giving.

GIVING THROUGH PUBLIC FOUNDATIONS

If you are clear about your causes and recipient organizations, it can be relatively easy to make donations directly. However, if you have a significant amount of capital you wish to protect for charitable giving, then one way to meet your giving goals is to channel your donations through a donor-advised account at one of many progressive social change foundations such as Tides and Tides Canada, whose mandate is to help donors support social change locally, nationally, or internationally.

An individual donor (or non-staffed family foundation) can establish a donor-advised fund (DAF), contributing money annually or endowing it and granting the annual investment income. Once the DAF is established (the donor receives a charitable receipt for the contribution), the donor advises the public foundation regarding which charities to support and for how much. The foundation offers customized services, including help in clarifying your values, building a strategy and goals, researching prospective grantees, site visits, and follow-up evaluations.

A donor-advised fund can be useful for donors who are:

- Granting at least $5,000 annually or endowing with at least $100,000.
- Needing administrative or program support in managing strategic grant-making (devising goals, doing due diligence, issuing checks, tracking receipts, etc.).
- Considering gifting appreciated securities or other non-monetary assets that might be used to fund multiple grants or an endowment.
- Seeking a quick, uncomplicated, and less expensive set-up than establishing one's own foundation, while enjoying access to helpful philanthropic counsel.
- Seeking anonymity (donor-assisted funds can be named or anonymous).
- Requiring support to manage their existing non-staffed private foundation.

> *Social change foundations "identify and screen potential grant recipients ... and in general they ensure that donor dollars are well spent ... Social change foundations can make giving easy and effective."*
> — Chuck Collins and Pam Rogers, *Robin Hood Was Right*[10]

MAKING THE WORLD A BETTER PLACE

Given the choice, we all want to make the world a better place — for ourselves, our neighbors, our children, and our grandchildren. The difficulty in a complex society is in aligning our day-to-day decisions and actions with our deeply held (but too often buried) values. We tend to underestimate how profound an impact we can have in helping to bring about positive change; it is exciting to consider the progress being made by dedicated people in the non-profit sector, despite current severe funding constraints. Giving strategically to non-profits, particularly those with a long-term social change mission, is rewarding for the giver, essential for the non-profit organizations, and fundamental to making the world a better place for us all.

FURTHER RESOURCES

While we relied on many sources including our own experience to write this chapter, we also drew from two excellent books. We would like to thank those authors:

Tracy Gary and Melissa Kohner, *Inspired Philanthropy: Your Step-by-Step Guide to Creating a Giving Plan,* Jossey-Bass, 2002.

Chuck Collins and Pam Rogers with Joan P. Garner, *Robin Hood Was Right: A Guide to Giving Your Money for Social Change,* W.W. Norton, 2000.

Space constraints prevent us providing a comprehensive resource listing, but the Tides Foundation (<www.tides.org>) and Tides Canada (<www.tidescanada.ca>) websites highlight many organizations and tools. The Tides family also offers donor education salons and workshops across North America with partners such as the Canadian Women's Foundation (<www.cdnwomen.org>). For further information on social change, see the Resources section at the end of this book.

Like good decision making about a lot of things, a certain amount of action in this area involves daring to make decisions that either might not turn out as you hope or, conversely, may yield more than anyone could have imagined. If your tolerance for risk is low, think about challenging yourself. Since what's at stake can potentially change lives, the returns can be huge.
— Tracy Gary and Melissa Kohner, *Inspired Philanthropy*[11]

AFTERWORD
WHERE DO WE GO FROM HERE?

"Would you tell me, please, which way I ought to
walk from here?"
"That depends a good deal on where you want to get
to," said the Cat.
"I don't much care where," said Alice.
"Then it doesn't matter which way you walk."
— LEWIS CARROLL, *ALICE IN WONDERLAND*

It matters which way we walk. But many of us are too busy to get
beyond good intentions. It's time to accept responsibility for our
own actions. Does this mean that we should give corporations a free
ride? That we should be responsible for their transgressions? Not at
all. But we own those corporations through our retirement portfolios and pension plans. And we interact with them every day as
employees, as consumers, as suppliers, and as communities. We have
clout. And we can use that to hold them accountable for their
impact on our society.

Apathy is a powerful negative force. By ignoring the situation we
implicitly support the status quo. You've heard it many times in this
book. If companies think you don't care, why should they respond?
When they know that you care — they have to change or become
financially unsustainable. Boycotts have shown us that. But they're
not charities, so they won't create green life-affirming products
made in reasonable working conditions by workers who are fed,
clothed, housed, and educated if consumers continue to go to big

box stores to buy the cheapest, sweatshop-produced, disposable products that they can find. They won't spend millions designing energy efficient vehicles that can never become a profitable part of their business if we keep buying SUVs and other energy hogs to drive our kids to ballet and pick up milk at the store.

Where do you go from here? Start with your investments — pure capital is a powerful force. You have to make informed decisions about investing anyway so add a little due diligence and ensure that you're leveraging your capital for social change. There's more and more evidence that you won't have to give up financial return to make a difference. By investing in socially responsible mutual funds that focus on shareholder activism, you can have an impact. If your retirement savings are in a pension fund, talk to the trustees of that fund. Let them know that you're concerned about long-term shareholder value. It's their job to be the stewards of your retirement benefits.

Take a good look at your consumption habits. I won't dwell on reducing consumption — you all know that doing with less will make the biggest difference of all. But if you spend hours researching the merits of a two versus three mega-pixel digital camera — try spending a few extra minutes checking out the company that manufactures it. Co-op America, IdealsWork, and other websites can help. Ask for recycled and buy recycled. Ask for organic and buy organic. Food is half as expensive as it was when I was a kid. Spend a little extra and support growers that care for the planet and give your kids a pesticide-free existence just for the heck of it.

Think you can't afford it? Remember when drinking water was free? By ignoring the damage we're doing to our watersheds, we've turned water into another "stock keeping unit" — just one more product on the shelves of our grocery stores. And all those agro-chemicals will eventually make land unsuitable for food production. Guess what'll happen to the cost of food then!

When possible, buy products that have undergone a certification process that incorporates environmental sustainability and social justice (Fair Trade, eco-certified, and so on). Call and send letters to companies telling them what you like and don't like about them and their products and services. And give your business to the ones that are responsive and interested in your perspective.

Give back to your community and to communities abroad. We can beat poverty. Find ways to help. Support the kinds of philanthropy that Tim Draimin and Drummond Pike talked about in Chapter Ten or take a percent or two less on your term deposit and support community investment programs that help build sustainable communities. Give back to your employer. Get them in touch with Canadian Business for Social Responsibility or Business for Social Responsibility in the US and show them that there is a path to social and environmental sustainability and ultimately greater financial sustainabilty. Tell everyone you know that there are solutions.

Picture a world where access to food, water, clean air, and human dignity are rights, not privileges. Where communities are free of HIV/AIDS and other deadly diseases. Where people can live and work in safe, clean conditions. We can create the kind of world that we want to live in, but only if we're prepared to be more engaged.

I hope that I've given you some resources to help you become part of the solution. We can have an impact on globalization. We must have an impact!

HELP!
RESOURCES FOR THE SOCIAL INVESTOR

OPTIONS FOR THE INVESTOR

To learn more about social investment options where you live, contact:

Social Investment Organization
<www.socialinvestment.ca>
A Canadian non-profit organization dedicated to social investing and to providing information, education, and support services.

Social Investment Forum
<www.socialinvest.org>
A US non-profit organization promoting the concept, practice and growth of social investing. Lots of good articles, contacts, and resources.

UK Social Investment Forum
<www.uksif.org>
UKSIF promotes and encourages the development and positive impact of social investing in the UK.

Co-op America
<www.coopamerica.org>
This site can help you to become a more conscious consumer and to make better decisions based on your core values.

RESOURCES FOR THE ACTIVE SHAREHOLDER

The following social investment fund companies filed or co-filed shareholder proposals in 2003.

Canada

Real Assets Investment Management
<www.realassets.ca>

Ethical Funds
<www.ethicalfunds.com>

Meritas Mutual Funds
<www.meritas.ca>

SHARE (Shareholder Association for Research and Education)
<www.share.ca>

Files shareholder resolutions on behalf of shareholders. Lists shareholder proposals filed and provides educational information for pension trustees, along with policy papers on corporate social responsibility.

United States

These fund companies filed or co-filed shareholder proposals in the US in 2003 (Source: ICCR website)

Real Assets Investment Management
<www.realassets.ca>

Ethical Funds
<www.ethicalfunds.com>

Trillium Asset Management
<www.trilliuminvest.com>

Calvert Asset Management
<www.calvertgroup.com>

Domini Social Investments
<www.domini.com>

Walden Asset Management
<www.waldenassetmgmt.com>

Boston Common Asset Management
<www.bostoncommonasset.com>

Women's Equity Mutual Fund
<www.womens-equity.com>

Clean Yield Asset Management
<www.cleanyield.com>

Progressive Investment Management
<www.progressiveinvestment.com>

Harrington Investments Inc.
<www.harringtoninvestments.com>

Carlisle Social Investments
<www.carlislesri.com>

ISIS Asset Management
<www.friendsis.com>

Citizens Funds
<www.efund.com>

RESOURCES FOR THE CONSUMER

Wood Products – Saving endangered forests

Smartwood
<www.smartwood.org>
A forest certification project of the Rainforest Alliance, this site is a clearinghouse for information on sustainable forestry and certified wood products.

Forest Certification Center
<www.certifiedwood.org>
Great resource for information on the different certification schemes; also lists certified forests and provides a consumer list of certified wood products.

Woodwise – Co-op America
<www.woodwise.org>
Part of Co-op America's suite of consumer websites, this site lists what products to buy and where to buy them as well as information on how to protect forests.

Markets Initiative
<www.oldgrowthfree.com>
A group of environmental organizations striving to create a market demand for sustainable forestry products. Lists suppliers and producers of old growth friendly wood and paper products.

Paper – Eco-friendly options

Magazine Paper Project
<www.ecopaperaction.org>
Encourages magazines to print on recycled paper.

Recycled Paper Coalition
<www.papercoalition.org>

Coalition of major American organizations combining their efforts to reduce office paper waste and to increase purchasing of environmentally preferred paper.

The Recycled Products Purchasing Cooperative
<www.recycledproducts.org>
A non-profit program that provides discounts on recycled paper and products to co-op members.

ReThink Paper
<www.rethinkpaper.org>
Site dedicated to reducing paper waste and encouraging the growth of recycled and alternative paper markets.

Tuna – One fish two fish red fish tuna fish

Earthtrust
<www.earthtrust.org/fsa.html>
Dolphin-safe tuna certification program.

Bananas – A bunch of positive changes

Rainforest Alliance
<www.rainforest-alliance.org>
Better Banana Project website. Describes initiatives and which companies are involved.

Banana Link
<www.bananalink.org.uk>
UK organization dedicated to creating sustainable production and ethical trade in bananas.

Fair Fruit
<www.web.net/fairfruit>
Canadian initiative working to increase awareness of Fair Trade issues and increase the amount of Fair Trade fruit available in Canada.

Chiquita
<www.chiquita.com>
Contains information on Chiquita's efforts to become certified.

Food and Agriculture Organization of the United Nations
<www.fao.org>
Great source for information and statistics about food production in developing countries and around the globe.

Fair Trade Coffee — Choosing a true brew

Oxfam Canada
<www.oxfam.ca/campaigns/fair Trade.htm>
Oxfam Canada's listing of Fair Trade coffee retailers in Canada.

TransFair Canada
<www.transfair.ca/coffee/retail. html>
Fair Trade Certification organization. Offers an extensive list of coffee retailers selling Fair Trade coffee in Canada, as well as Fair Trade retailers for tea, cocoa and sugar.

The Fairtrade Foundation
<www.fairtrade.org.uk>
Homepage of the Fair Trade movement. Contains information on Fair Trade practices, guidelines, and producers for coffee, tea, bananas, and other products.

Chocolate — Products that won't leave a bitter taste

La Siembra Co-op
<www.lasiembra.com>
A co-op selling organic, Fair Trade cocoa products.

Global Exchange
<www.globalexchange.org/cam paigns/fairtrade/cocoa/>
Human rights organization providing information on chocolate production and on which products to buy.

Divine Chocolate

Fair Trade chocolate bar company in the UK created and part-owned by cocoa farmers in Ghana.

TransFair USA
<www.transfairusa.org>
Website has information on Fair Trade chocolate, coffee and tea in the US.

Fairtrade Federation
<www.fairtradefederation.com>
An American association of Fair Trade wholesalers, retailers, and producers committed to Fair Trade policies.

Rugs — Why it's good to have a mark on your rug

RUGMARK
<www.rugmark.org>
Website where retailers and importers can sign on and where consumers can discover which companies produce rugs that have been certified as made without child labor.

No More Sweatshops — Supporting responsible labor practices

Co-op America
<www.sweatshops.org>
Dedicated to ending sweatshop

and child labor. Contains information on companies that are responsible and shows how to pressure companies to act responsibly.

Fisheries — Netting sustainable seafood

Marine Stewardship Council
<www.msc.org>
Lists certified fisheries and where certified products can be bought.

Informed Consumer Choices

IdealsWork Inc.
<www.IdealsWork.com>
Provides rankings for companies and products based on several different ethical categories such as labor issues, environment, women's issues, etc.

Ethical Consumer
<www.ethicalconsumer.org>
Information on the ethical history of companies as well as current boycotts.

CorpWatch
<www.corpwatch.org>
Dedicated to holding corporations accountable. Includes a step-by-step guide on how to research the ethical history of a company.

Responsible Shopper – Co-op America
<www.responsibleshopper.org>
Co-op America website that provides consumers with information on the ethical standing of companies, brands, and products.

Ethical Product Listings

Green Pages On-line — Co-op America
<www.greenpages.org>
On-line directory of businesses and products that Co-op America has screened as being socially and environmentally responsible.

Ecomall
<www.ecomall.com>
"Earth's largest environmental shopping center." Searches hundreds of websites to provide lists of environmentally friendly products.

Green Seal
<www.greenseal.org>
Non-profit organization that identifies and promotes services and products that are environmentally friendly.

Recycling Markets
<www.recyclingmarkets.net>

For-fee service that provides a comprehensive list of recycled products in North America.

Learn About Current Boycotts

Boycott Action News — Co-op America
<www.boycotts.org>
Site hosted by Co-op America that lists current boycotts and provides information on how to organize a boycott.

Be a Virtual Activist

Net Action
<www.netaction.org>
Contains information on how to use the Internet for outreach and advocacy, as well as articles and resources about virtual activism.

Action! Network
<www.actionnetwork.org>
Website designed to encourage and aid virtual activists. Provides links to other activists and networks.

COMMUNITY INVESTMENT RESOURCES
Trade Associations

Community investing is one of the pillars of social investing, so if you are interested in investigating community investment opportunities, the following social investing trade associations are a great place to start.

Social Investment Organization (Canada): <www.socialinvestment.ca>

Social Investment Forum (US): <www.socialinvest.org>

UK Social Investment Forum (UK): <www.uksif.org>

Organizations

International Association of Investors in the Social Economy (Europe) <www.inaise.org> A network of socially and environmentally oriented financial institutions at the global level. Provides information about micro-finance and social banking programs.

National Federation of Community Development Credit Unions (US) <www.natfed.org> Community development credit unions (CDCUs) dedicated to revitalizing low-income communities. Includes educational information on how to start a CDCU as well as advocacy strategies.

Discussion Groups

Social Bank List Serve Send an email to sympa@globenet.org. Write in the body of the message: "subscribe social-banking" along with your first name and last name.

Community Development Banking List Subscribe at <www.alternatives.org/cdblist.htm> Bills itself as the best community development banking resource in cyberspace. Run by Cornell University and Alternatives Credit Union.

Financial Institutions and Intermediaries

The following institutions are leaders in social/community investment programs:

Vancouver City Savings Credit Union <www.vancity.com>

Triodos Bank <www.triodos.com>

ShoreBank Corporation <www.shorebankcorp.com>

*Real Assets Investment
Management*
<www.realassets.ca>

Meritas Mutual Funds
<www.meritas.ca>

Calvert Foundation
<www.calvertfoundation.org>

CSR RESOURCES

These websites are the top picks
of each of the CSR leaders
interviewed in Chapter Nine.

Business in the Community
<www.bitc.org.uk>
Dedicated to corporate social
responsibility and best business
practices. This site offers statistics, case studies, and toolkits
for companies.

Business for Social Responsibility
<www.bsr.org>
Here you'll find tools, training,
and advisory services to make
corporate social responsibility an
integral part of business operations and strategies.

*Canadian Business for Social
Responsibility* <www.cbsr.ca>
One stop CSR shop for
Canadians. Featuring tools,
training news, and information

for those interested in corporate
social responsibility.

Dow Jones Sustainability Index
<www.sustainability-index.com>
Detailed information on
methodology, plus guidebooks,
key facts, and the components
of the holdings in the DJSI
STOXX index.

Global Reporting Initiative
(GRI)
<www.globalreporting.org>
This site provides the reporting
framework and guidelines as
well as list of organizational
stakeholders that have signed
on to the GRI.

Social Funds
<www.socialfunds.com>
Features complete, in-depth
information on SRI mutual
funds, community investments,
corporate research, shareowner
actions, along with daily social
investment news.

Sustainable Asset Management
<www.sam-group.com>
Provides corporate, financial,
and sustainability information
on companies that are
"Sustainability Leaders."
Business and Human Rights

Resource Centre
<www.business-humanrights.org>
Everything and anything you
want to know about international human rights.

Ethical Corporation On-line
<www.ethicalcorp.com>
News, analysis, and events relating to global corporate citizenship.

Publications

Tomorrow Magazine
Global sustainable business
magazine.

CSR News
<www.csrwire.com>
The leading source of corporate
responsibility and sustainability

provides press releases, reports,
and news.

Excel Partnership
<www.excelpartnership.ca>
Excellence in corporate environmental leadership. A group of
major Canadian corporations,
committed to environmental
and sustainable development.

*World Business Council for
Sustainable Development*
<www.wbcsd.org>
A coalition of 165 international
companies united by a shared
commitment to sustainable
development via the three pillars of economic growth, ecological balance, and social
progress.

ENDNOTES

CHAPTER ONE

1. Anita Roddick, *Business As Unusual,* Thorsens/HarperCollins, 2001.

2. Oxfam International, *Mugged: Poverty in Your Coffee Cup,* Report prepared for Oxfam International, 2002.

3 Pascal Couchepin, from an opening speech delivered to the *World Economic Forum,* Davos, January 2003, [on-line], [cited June 2003]. <www.edi.admin.ch/discours-dfie/2003/030123wef-davos-e.pdf>.

4. SustainAbility and the United Nations Environment Program (UNEP), *Trust Us: Global Reporters Survey of Corporate Sustainability Reporting, 2002* [on-line], [cited June 2003]. <www.sustainability.com/news/press-room/trust-us-Nov-2002.asp>.

5. Lester R. Brown, *Plan B: Rescuing a Planet Under Stress and a Civilization in Trouble,* W.W. Norton, 2003.

6. Lester R. Brown, *Plan B: Rescuing a Planet Under Stress and a Civilization in Trouble,* W.W. Norton, 2003. p. 1.

CHAPTER TWO

1. M. Orlitzky, F.L. Schmidt, and S.L. Rynes, "Corporate Social and Financial Performance: A Meta-Analysis," *Organizational Studies,* 24:3, 2003, pp. 403–442.

2. J. Margolis and J.P. Walsh, *Misery Loves Companies: Whither Social Initiatives by Business,* Unpublished paper, Harvard University, June 2001.

3. Ronald M. Roman, Sefa Hayibor, and Bradley R. Agle, "The Relationship Between Social and Financial Performance," *Business and Society,* Vol 38, No. 1, March 1999.

4. Jeff Frooman, "Socially Irresponsible and Illegal Behaviour and Shareholder Wealth: a Meta-Analysis of Event Studies," *Business and Society,* Vol 36, No 3, 1997.

5. Kenneth Labich, "The New Crisis in Business Ethics," *Fortune,* April 20, 1993.

6. Curtis C. Verschoor and Elizabeth A. Murphy, "The Strong Direct Link Between CSR and Profitability: The Best Corporate Citizens Do Outperform the Remaining S & P 500 Companies." From a presentation by Curtis C. Verschoor at *SRI In The Rockies,* Colorado Springs, Oct 20, 2002.

7. Anne Papmehl, "Sustainable Development and Your Portfolio," *Benefits Canada,* 2002.

8. Sustainable Assets Management, [on-line], [cited June 2003], <www.sam-group.com>, <www.sam-group.com/e/susindex/susindex.cfm>.

9. KLD Research and Analytics, *Benchmarks: The Domini 400 Social Index,* [on-line], [cited June 2003], <www.kld.com/benchmarks/dsi.html>.

10. Michael Jantzi Research Associates, [on-line], [cited June 2003], <www.mjra-jsi.com>.

11. Social Investment Forum, [on-line], [cited June 2003], <www.socialinvest.org>.

12. Tim Smith, "SRI NEWS: Socially Responsible Funds Earning Top Marks Edged Even Higher in 2002," *GreenMoneyJournal.com* [on-line], [cited June 2003], <www.greenmoneyjournal.com/article.mpl?newsletterid=23&articleid=240>

13. Alisa Gravitz, "SRI NEWS: Socially Responsible Funds Earning Top Marks Edged Even Higher in 2002," *GreenMoneyJournal.com* [on-line], [cited June 2003] <www.greenmoneyjournal.com/article.mpl?newsletterid=23&articleid=240>.

14. PricewaterhouseCoopers, *5th Annual Global CEO Survey, 2001,* [on-line], [cited June 2003], <www.pwcglobal.com>, <www.pwcglobal.com/fr/pwc_pdf/pwc_ceo_2001.pdf>.

15. Burson-Marsteller, *The Responsible Century: Summary of an International Opinion Leader Survey on Corporate Social*

Responsibility, 2001, [on-line], [cited June 2003], <www.pwblf.org>, <www.iblf.org/csr/CSRWebAssist.nsf/content/f1d2a3b4c5b6.html>, <www.iblf.org/csr/ CSR WebAssist.nsf/550d4b46b29f68a6852568660081f938/8525 68eb00754e108525690d0058d6b7/$FILE/CSRart.pdf>.

CHAPTER THREE

1. Paul Hawken, "Natural Capitalism," *Mother Jones* magazine, March/April 1997. <www.mindfully.org/Sustainability/Hawken-Natural-Capitalism.htm>.

2. US Department of Agriculture, [on-line], [cited July 2003], <www.ers.usda.gov>.

3. Josh Garrison, [on-line], [cited July 2003}, <www.cisco.com>.

CHAPTER FOUR

1. European Wind Energy Association, [on-line], [cited June 2003], <www.ewea.org>.

2. Joint European Wind Energy Association and Greenpeace Report, [on-line], [cited June 2003], <www.ewea.org>.

3. Maude Barlow and Tony Clarke, *Blue Gold: The Fight to Stop the Corporate Theft of the World's Water,* New Press, 2002.

4. Diane Raines Ward, *Water Wars: Drought, Flood, Folly, and the Politics of Thirst,* Riverhead Books, 2002.

5. Brian Natrass and Mary Altomare, *The Natural Step for Business,* New Society Publishers, 1999.

6. Interface, *Getting There, 2002,* [on-line], [cited June 2003], <www.interfaceinc.com/getting_there>.

CHAPTER FIVE

1. Tim Smith, "Report: 2003 Proxy Season Expected To Set Records, With CEO Pay and Global Warming Among Top Issues," *Social Investment Forum News* [on-line], [cited June 2003], <www.irrc.org/company/02122003_CEOPay.html>, <www.shareholderaction.org>.

2. Shareholder Association for Research and Education (SHARE), [on-line], [cited June 2003], <www.share.ca/files/pdfs/ 2003% 20Shareholder%20Proposals11.pdf>.

CHAPTER SIX

1. "Boycotting Corporate America," *The Economist,* May 26, 1990, pp. 69–70.

2. Sankar Sen, Zeynep Gurhan-Canli, and Vicki Morwitz, "Withholding Consumption: A Social Dilemma Perspective on Consumer Boycotts," *Journal of Consumer Research,* December 2001.

3. *The Columbia Encyclopedia,* 6th edition, Columbia University Press, 2003. [on-line], [cited June 2003], <http://www.bartleby.com/65/bo/boycott.html>.

4. John Keith Forsyth, *Customer Attitudes Towards Environmentally Sound Wood Products in Three British Columbian Home Improvement Markets,* Unpublished master's thesis, University of British Columbia, 1997.

5. IBM Consulting Services, *A Greenward Shift in the Market for Forest Products from British Columbia,* 2002.

6. Anil Hira and Jared Ferrie, *Fair Trade: An Idea Whose Time Has Come,* Paper, Simon Fraser University, May 15, 2003, p.14.

7. *Fish Facts: Fish and the Environment* [on-line], [cited June 2003] <www.msc.org>

8. *The History of the Northern Cod Fishery,* [on-line], [cited June 2003], <http://collections.ic.gc.ca/cod/>.

9. Environics, *The Millennium Poll on Corporate Social Responsibility,* Conducted in cooperation with the Prince of Wales Business Leaders Forum and the Conference Board, 1999.

10. Green Mountain Energy Company, Opinion Research Corporation Survey, 2002. Original Source: American Demographics, September 2002.

11. Cooperative Development Services, *Organic Dairy, Poultry, and Eggs: Market Reviews and Competitive Analyses,* 2002.

12.. IdealsWork Inc., [on-line], [cited June 2003], <www.idealswork.com>.

CHAPTER SEVEN

1. Tessa Hebb, "The Challenge of Labor's Capital Strategy," *Social Policy,* April 2001.

2.   Statistics Canada, Quarterly Estimates of Trusteed Pension Funds, first quarter 2002, Vol. 30 No 1 [on-line], [cited June 2003], <www.statcan.ca/english/IPS/Data/74-001-XIB.htm>.

3.   CalPERS, *Facts at a Glance,* Corporate Governance, May 2003.

4.   Diane Del Guercio and Jennifer Hawkins, "The Motivation and Impact of Pension Fund Activism," *Journal of Financial Economics,* 1999.

5.   NYC Comptroller, [on-line], [cited June 2003], <www.comptroller.nyc.gov>.

6.   Chris Gribben and Leon Olsen, *Will UK Pension Funds Become More Responsible? A survey of member nominated trustees,* Ashridge Centre for Business and Society, 2003.

7.   Stephen Viederman, *New Directions in Fiduciary Responsibility.* Expanded version of remarks made at the meeting of the International Interfaith Investment Group, sponsored by the Alliance of Religions and Conservation (UK), New York, June 20, 2002; and at the Green Mountain SRI Summit: A Forum on Environmental, Social, Faith-Based & Sustainable Investing, Stowe, Vermont, September 9, 2002. Further information can be found at <www.theglobalacademy.org/SV%20Paper3_IFR.asp> [on-line], [cited June 2003].

8.   Gil Yaron, "The Responsible Pension Trustee: Re-Interpreting the Principles of Prudence and Loyalty in the Context of Socially Responsible Institutional Investing," *Estates, Trusts and Pension Journal,* 305. 2001.

CHAPTER EIGHT

1.   *Enterprising Communities: Wealth Beyond Welfare,* Report to the Chancellor of the Exchequer from the Social Investment Task, October 2000, <www.enterprising-communities.org.uk/rpt-cont.shml>.

2.   For additional information see Social Investment Forum, "Increasing Investment in Communities: A Community Investment Guide for Investment Professionals and Institutions," 2000, [on-line], [cited June 2003], <www.socialinvest.org/areas/general/investors/institutions.htm>.

CHAPTER NINE

1.   Canadian Business for Social Responsibility, *Building a Corporate Social Responsibility Plan: Using a Systems Approach,* [on-line], [cited June 2003], <www.cbsr.bc.ca>.

2.   James C. Collins, *From Good to Great: Why Some Companies Make the Leap ... and Others Don't*, HarperCollins, 2001.

CHAPTER TEN

1.   The Center on Philanthropy at Indiana University, *Giving USA 2002*, AAFRC Trust For Philanthropy, 2002.

2.   Katherine Scott, *Funding Matters: The Impact of Canada's New Funding Regime on Nonprofit and Voluntary Organizations*, Summary Report, Canadian Council on Social Development, 2003, pp. 2, 4. Publication is available at <www.ccsd.ca/pubs/2003/fm/>.

3.   Tracy Gary and Melissa Kohner, *Inspired Philanthropy: Your Step-by-Step Guide to Creating a Giving Plan*, Jossey-Bass, 2002, pp. 3–4.

4.   Christopher Mogil and Anne Slepian, *Welcome to Philanthropy: Resources for Individuals and Families Exploring Social Change Giving*, National Network of Grantmakers, 1997, p. 3.

5.   Nicole Etchart and Lee Davis, "Prophets for Nonprofits?" *Alliance*, Vol. 7 No. 2, June 2002, p. 22.

6.   J. Gregory Dees, "The Meaning of Social Entrepreneurship," <http://hcs.harvard.edu/~sec/SocialEnterpriseTrackApplication Guidelines.doc>.

7.   Sources for graph: *Giving USA 2001*, The Center on Philanthropy at Indiana University, AAFRC Trust For Philanthropy 2001, and *2000 National Survey on Giving, Volunteering and Participating*, Ketchum Canada estimates, 2000.

8.   Chuck Collins and Pam Rogers with Joan P. Garner, *Robin Hood Was Right: A Guide to Giving Your Money for Social Change*, W.W. Norton, 2000, p. 77.

9.   Chuck Collins and Pam Rogers with Joan P. Garner, *Robin Hood Was Right: A Guide to Giving Your Money for Social Change*, W.W. Norton, 2000, p. 76-77.

10. Chuck Collins and Pam Rogers with Joan P. Garner, *Robin Hood Was Right: A Guide to Giving Your Money for Social Change*, W.W. Norton, 2000, p. 170.

11. Tracy Gary and Melissa Kohner, *Inspired Philanthropy: Your Step-by-Step Guide to Creating a Giving Plan*, Jossey-Bass, 2002, p. 83.

GLOSSARY

BBP: The Better Banana Project, A project initiated in 1991 by the Rainforest Alliance and its partners to reduce the negative environmental impacts of banana cultivation and improve working conditions on farms. For more information see <www.rainforest-alliance.org>.

CalPERS: California Public Employees' Retirement System. Provides retirement and health benefit services to more than 1.3 million Californians. As the largest retirement system in the US, CalPERS has long been a leader in the corporate governance movement. For more information see <www.calpers-governance.org>.

CBSR: Canadian Business for Social Responsibility. As Canada's leading voice for corporate social responsibility, CBSR's goal is to support business in their effort to implement higher standards of social and environmental responsibility. CBSR's member companies are among Canada's leaders and as such, are committed to developing, sharing. and implementing corporate social responsibility best practices. For more information see <www.cbsr.ca>.

CERES Principles: Coalition for Environmentally Responsible Economies. A set of principles that corporations can adopt to publicly affirm their commitment to being responsible, accountable stewards of the environment in every facet of their business, from waste management and energy conservation to employee safety and public reporting. For more information see <www.ceres.org>.

CII: Council of Institutional Investors. An organization of large public, labor funds, and corporate pension funds which seeks to address investment issues that affect the size or security of plan assets. Its objectives are to encourage member funds, as major shareholders, to take an active role in protecting plan assets and to help members increase return on their investments as part of their fiduciary obligations. For more information see <www.cii.org>.

CSR: Corporate Social Responsibility. A company's commitment to operating in an economically and environmentally sustainable manner while recognizing the interests of its stakeholders. Stakeholders include investors, customers, employees, business partners, local communities, the environment, and society at large.

DJSGI: Dow Jones Sustainability Group Index. Created by the Dow Jones Index and Sustainable Asset Management, the DJSGI represents the top ten percent of the leading sustainability companies in the world and represents over 300 companies. For more information see <www.sustainability-index.com>.

DSI: Domini 400 Social Index. An index of 400 primarily large-capitalization US corporations selected based on a wide range of social and environmental criteria. For more information see <www.domini.com>.

EEO: Equal Employment Opportunity. The system of laws prohibiting employment discrimination based on race, color, religion, sex, age, disability, political affiliation, or national origin.

EPI: Ethical Purchasing Index. Developed by the Co-operative Bank in the UK, the Ethical Purchasing Index attempts to measure growth in the marketplace for ethical goods and services.

FSC: Forest Stewardship Council. The Forest Stewardship Council is an international non-profit organization founded in 1993 to support environmentally appropriate, socially beneficial, and economically viable management of the world's forests. For more information see <www.fscoax.org>.

Global Sullivan Principles: The objectives of the Global Sullivan Principles are to support economic, social, and political justice by companies wherever they do business; to support human rights and to encourage equal opportunity at all levels of employment, including racial and gender diversity on decision making committees and boards; to train and advance disadvantaged workers for technical, supervisory, and management opportunities; and to assist in creating greater tolerance and understanding among peoples; thereby helping to improve the quality of life for communities, workers, and children with dignity and equality. For more information see <www.globalsullivanprinciples.org>.

GRI: Global Reporting Initiative. A multi-stakeholder process and independent institution whose mission is to develop and disseminate globally applicable Sustainability Reporting Guidelines. For more information see <www.globalreporting.org>.

GIC: Guaranteed Investment Certificate. A deposit investment security sold by Canadian banks and trust companies.

ICCR: Interfaith Center for Corporate Responsibility. A leader of the corporate social responsibility movement in the United States, ICCR represents 275 faith-based institutional investors, including national denominations, religious communities, pension funds, endowments, hospital corporations, economic development funds, and publishing companies working to press companies to be socially and environmentally responsible. For more information see <www.iccr.org>.

ILO: International Labor Organization. The UN's specialized agency which seeks the promotion of social justice and internationally recognized human and labor rights. For more information see <www.ilo.org>.

IRRC: Investor Responsibility Research Center. An independent research organization that has been the leading source of high quality, impartial information on corporate governance and social responsibility issues. For more information see <www.irrc.org>.

ISS: Institutional Shareholder Services, Inc. The world's leading provider of proxy voting and corporate governance services. For more information see <www.issproxy.com>.

JSI: Jantzi Social Index.® A socially screened, market capitalization-weighted common stock index modeled on the Standard and Poor/Toronto Stock Exchange 60 (then the S&P/TSE 60). The JSI® consists of 60 Canadian companies that pass a set of broadly-based social and environmental screens. For more information see <www.mjra-jsi.com/jsi>.

KAIROS: Canadian Ecumenical Justice Initiatives. Established in 1991, KAIROS brings together the work of ten individual inter-church coalitions. This group is dedicated to promoting human rights, justice, and peace, viable human development, and universal solidarity among the peoples of the Earth. For more information see <www.kairoscanada.org>.

LOHAS: Lifestyles of Health and Sustainability. Describes a US$226.8 billion marketplace for goods and services that appeal to consumers who value health, the environment, social justice, personal development, and sustainable living. These consumers are variously referred to as Cultural Creatives or as LOHAS Consumers and represent a sizable group in the United States. Fore more information see <www.lohasjournal.com>.

McBride Principles: A corporate code of conduct for US companies doing business in Northern Ireland, consisting of nine fair employment, affirmative action principles.

MJRA: Michael Jantzi Research Associates. Provides a full range of social investment research and support services to institutional clients and financial professionals who integrate social and environmental criteria into their investment decisions. For more information see <www.mjra-jsi.com>.

MSC: Marine Stewardship Council. The MSC is an independent, global, non-profit organization set up to find a solution to the problem of overfishing. The council has developed an environmental standard for sustainable and well-managed fisheries following worldwide consultation with scientists, fisheries experts, environmental organizations, and other people with a strong interest in preserving fish stocks for the future. For more information see <www.msc.org>.

NYCERS: New York City Employees Retirement System

OECD: Organization of Economic Cooperation and Development. The OECD groups 30 member countries sharing a commitment to democratic government and the market economy. With active relationships with some 70 other countries, NGOs and civil society, it has a global reach. The OECD plays a prominent role in fostering good governance in the public service and in corporate activity. Best known for its publications and its statistics, its work covers economic and social issues. For more information see
<www.oecd.org>

Real Assets Investment Management Inc.: The first full-service investment management firm in Canada to focus entirely on social impact investing. Real Assets is a leading proponent of proactive shareholder strategies that push companies to improve the way they manage social, environmental, and ethical factors. Along with managed portfolios and pooled funds for institutional investors, in 2003 the firm launched two cutting-edge mutual funds aimed at individual investors: the Social Leaders Fund and the Social Impact Balanced Fund. For more information visit <www.realassets.ca>.

RPS: Renewable Portfolio Standards. Renewable Portfolio Standards (RPS) are state policies mandating a state to generate a percent of its electricity from renewable sources. Each state has a choice of how to fulfill this mandate using a combination of renewable energy sources, including wind, solar, biomass, geothermal, or other renewable sources. Some RPSs will specify the technology mix, while others leave it up to the market

RRSP Registered Retirement Savings Plan. An RRSP is a government-approved program that is designed to encourage Canadians to save for their retirement by providing powerful tax reduction options.

S & P 500: Standard and Poor's 500 Index. Widely regarded as the standard for measuring large-cap US stock market performance, this popular index includes a representative sample of leading companies in leading industries. The S & P 500 is used by 97 percent of US money managers and pension plan sponsors. More than $1 trillion is indexed to the S & P 500. For more information see <www.spglobal.com>.

SHARE: The Shareholder Association for Research and Education. A not-for-profit organization helping Canadian pension funds to build sound investment practices, to protect the interests of plan beneficiaries, and to contribute to a just and healthy society.

SIF: Social Investment Forum. A US nonprofit organization promoting the concept, practice, and growth of social investing. For more information see <www.socialinvest.org>.

SIO: Social Investment Organization. A Canadian nonprofit organization dedicated to social investing and to providing information, education, and support services. For more information see <www.socialinvestment.ca>.

SRI: Socially Responsible Investment/ Social Investing. Making investment decisions that integrate personal values, concerns for society, and financial needs.

TCCR: Taskforce on the Churches and Corporate Responsibility. An ecumenical coalition of the major churches in Canada. For more information see <www.web.net/~tccr/>.

WEF: World Economic Forum. The World Economic Forum is an independent international organization committed to improving the state of the world. The forum provides a collaborative framework for the world's leaders to address global issues, engaging particularly its corporate members in global citizenship. For more information <www.weforum.org>.

INDEX

ABOUT THE AUTHOR

Deb Abbey is the founder and CEO of Real Assets, the first investment management firm in Canada to focus exclusively on social impact investing. Deb's diverse background gives her a unique insight into how business activities relate to social and environmental issues; she has been an entrepreneur, a social worker and Project Director for the David Suzuki Foundation. Deb became a financial advisor in 1995 and quickly established a thriving practice by helping individuals, charitable foundations and other institutions address social issues along with their financial concerns. Now, as portfolio manager for Real Assets social impact mutual funds, and one of Canada's leading experts and speakers on social investing and shareholder activism, Deb can more fully express her true vocation: leveraging invested capital to create a more just, sustainable world. Deb is co-author with social researcher Michael Jantzi of *The 50 Best Ethical Stocks for Canadians*.

If you have enjoyed *Global Profit AND Global Justice,*
you might also enjoy other

BOOKS TO BUILD A NEW SOCIETY

Our books provide positive solutions for people who want to
make a difference. We specialize in:

Environment and Justice • Conscientious Commerce
Sustainable Living • Ecological Design and Planning
Natural Building & Appropriate Technology • New Forestry
Educational and Parenting Resources • Nonviolence
Progressive Leadership • Resistance and Community

New Society Publishers

ENVIRONMENTAL BENEFITS STATEMENT

New Society Publishers has chosen to produce this book on Enviro 100, recycled paper made with **100% post consumer waste**, processed chlorine free, and old growth free.

For every 5,000 books printed, New Society saves the following resources:[1]

30	Trees
2,728	Pounds of Solid Waste
3,002	Gallons of Water
3,916	Kilowatt Hours of Electricity
4,960	Pounds of Greenhouse Gases
21	Pounds of HAPs, VOCs, and AOX Combined
8	Cubic Yards of Landfill Space

---

[1]Environmental benefits are calculated based on research done by the Environmental Defense Fund and other members of the Paper Task Force who study the environmental impacts of the paper industry.

For more information on this environmental benefits statement, or to inquire about environmentally friendly papers, please contact New Leaf Paper – info@newleafpaper.com Tel: 888 • 989 • 5323.

For a full list of NSP's titles, please call **1-800-567-6772** *or check out our web site at:*

www.newsociety.com

NEW SOCIETY PUBLISHERS